Negative and Positive Effects of Rejections in Online Product Testing Programs

Kira Louisa Küpper

Negative and Positive Effects of Rejections in Online Product Testing Programs

Springer

Kira Louisa Küpper
Bergische Universität Wuppertal
Velbert, Germany

This doctoral dissertation was accepted by the Faculty of Business and Economics – Schumpeter School of Business and Economics – at the University of Wuppertal.

ISBN 978-3-658-49276-2 ISBN 978-3-658-49277-9 (eBook)
https://doi.org/10.1007/978-3-658-49277-9

Translation from the German language edition: "Negative und positive Effekte von Absagen in Online-Produkttester-Programmen" by Kira Louisa Küpper, © Der/die Herausgeber bzw. der/die Autor(en), exklusiv lizenziert an Springer Fachmedien Wiesbaden GmbH, ein Teil von Springer Nature 2024. Published by Springer Fachmedien Wiesbaden. All Rights Reserved.

This book is a translation of the original German edition "Negative und positive Effekte von Absagen in Online-Produkttester-Programmen" by Kira Louisa Küpper, published by Springer Fachmedien Wiesbaden GmbH in 2024. The translation was done with the help of an artificial intelligence machine translation tool. A subsequent human revision was done primarily in terms of content, so that the book will read stylistically differently from a conventional translation. Springer Nature works continuously to further the development of tools for the production of books and on the related technologies to support the authors.

This Springer imprint is published by the registered company Springer Fachmedien Wiesbaden GmbH, part of Springer Nature.
The registered company address is: Abraham-Lincoln-Str. 46, 65189 Wiesbaden, Germany

Foreword

Online product testing programs are an increasingly popular marketing tool, as they are considered an effective method for collecting customer feedback and generating online customer reviews. Within these programs, customers are asked to test products and subsequently provide evaluations. In return, they are allowed to keep the test product. Since the opportunity to receive products free of charge is an attractive offer for many customers, the number of applications often exceeds the available test products. As a result, some applicants receive rejections.

To date, little is known about the effects these rejections may have on unsuccessful applicants and, consequently, on companies themselves. This dissertation addresses this issue by analyzing the impact of rejections within online product testing programs on the behavior of rejected applicants. Dr. Küpper formulates hypotheses regarding both the positive and negative effects of rejection on purchase intention and the intention to spread negative word-of-mouth. Furthermore, she explores the underlying psychological mechanisms driving these effects and empirically tests her hypotheses. Dr. Küpper's dissertation employs both qualitative and quantitative methods, drawing on extensive experimental and non-experimental data. Through her research, she addresses the following research questions:

1. Which psychological theories can explain the behavior of rejected applicants in online product testing programs?
2. How does rejection within the context of an online product testing program influence the purchasing behavior and willingness to recommend among rejected applicants?

3. Do product price and the number of rejections play a role in the behavior of rejected applicants?
4. Through which psychological mechanisms can the behavior of rejected applicants be explained?
5. What implications arise from the findings of these studies?

Dr. Küpper's work provides important insights for the management of online product testing programs. Although rejections in the context of product tests can increase purchase intention, there are also negative consequences such as the spread of negative word-of-mouth. The findings of this dissertation are therefore significant for both marketing research and practice. It is therefore worthwhile to read and engage with this work.

Prof. Dr. Ina Garnefeld

Preface

This dissertation was written during my tenure as a research associate at the Chair of Business Administration, with a focus on Service Management, at the Schumpeter School of Business and Economics, University of Wuppertal. Numerous individuals have made significant contributions to the successful completion of my doctoral studies, and I would like to express my gratitude to them here.

My special thanks go to my doctoral advisor, Prof. Dr. Ina Garnefeld, who gave me the opportunity to pursue my doctorate at her department. Throughout my time at the department, I developed both professionally and personally, and her ongoing support made this dissertation possible in the first place. She consistently enabled me to participate in international conferences and colloquia, allowing me to continuously advance my work.

Further thanks go to my second examiner, Prof. Dr. Tobias Langner, whose valuable comments in numerous doctoral colloquia have made a significant contribution.

I would also like to thank Professor Dr. Christine Volkmann, Professor Dr. Stephan Zielke, and Professor Dr. Peter Witt for their participation as members of my examination committee.

I had a particularly special time during my doctoral studies in Rostock. I would like to sincerely thank Prof. Dr. Lena Steinhoff for the invitation and the several-week research stay. During this period, I was able to further develop my methodological skills and received valuable input for my dissertation.

I would also like to thank the participants of the numerous dissertation workshops, doctoral seminars, and conferences. Presenting this work to a professional audience has always led to interesting discussions and improvements.

My time at the department was significantly shaped by my wonderful colleagues. I would like to thank Lisa Hanf, Dr. Katharina Kessing, Dr. Tabea Tesch, and Dr. Ann-Kathrin Grötschel for creating a pleasant working environment and for always being available to listen to questions and concerns.

My deepest gratitude goes to my family and friends. My parents Monika and Markus, my brother Leon, my sister-in-law Janina Louisa, and my husband Moritz have supported me at every stage and, through their trust in me and my work, contributed to this success. I could always draw the motivation I needed from them. My friends, especially Laura, Nils, Anja, and Raphaël, have accompanied me throughout this journey and have always provided unwavering support.

This work is dedicated to them.

Dr. Kira Louisa Küpper

Gender Statement

All personal designations in this dissertation are intended to be inclusive of all genders. For the sake of readability, gendered language forms—male, female, and diverse (m/f/d)—are not used simultaneously; instead, the generic masculine form is applied. Female and other gender identities are explicitly included wherever relevant to the context.

Contents

1 Introduction . . . 1
- 1.1 Relevance of the Topic for Marketing Research and Practice . . . 1
- 1.2 Objectives and Research Questions . . . 4
- 1.3 Structure of the Research . . . 4

2 Conceptual Foundations . . . 7
- 2.1 Online Product Testing Programs . . . 7
  - 2.1.1 Definition of Terms . . . 7
  - 2.1.2 Differentiation from Related Concepts . . . 10
  - 2.1.3 State of Research . . . 13
    - 2.1.3.1 Mechanisms of Product Sampling . . . 13
    - 2.1.3.2 Design Features of a Product Sampling Campaign . . . 16
    - 2.1.3.3 Effects of Online Product Testing . . . 18
- 2.2 Rejections . . . 22
  - 2.2.1 Definition of Terms . . . 22
  - 2.2.2 State of Research . . . 23
    - 2.2.2.1 Effects of Rejections . . . 23
    - 2.2.2.2 Influencing Factors on the Impact of Rejections . . . 30
- 2.3 Summary Assessment of the Conceptual Foundations . . . 35

3 Development of the Research Model . . . 37
- 3.1 Exploratory Qualitative Survey . . . 37
  - 3.1.1 Study Objective . . . 38
  - 3.1.2 Rationale for the Research Design . . . 38

3.1.3 Implementation 39
3.1.4 Sample Selection and Composition 41
3.1.5 Analysis of Results 42
3.1.5.1 Evaluation Method 42
3.1.5.2 Results 43
3.2 Theoretical Foundations 47
3.2.1 Attribution Theory 48
3.2.2 Commitment-Consistency Principle 51
3.3 Derivation of the Hypotheses 54
3.3.1 Negative Effects of a Rejection 54
3.3.2 Positive Effects of a Rejection 57
3.3.3 Moderating Effect of the Test Product's Price 59
3.3.4 Effect of the Number of Rejections 60
3.3.5 Summary of Hypotheses and Overview of the Research Model 62

4 Empirical Study 65
4.1 Overview of the Studies 65
4.2 Justification of the Research Designs 66
4.3 Study 1—Consequences of Rejections and the Role of Product Price 67
4.3.1 Study Objective 67
4.3.2 Study Design 68
4.3.3 Implementation 68
4.3.4 Recruitment and Composition of the Sample 69
4.3.5 Operationalization of Variables 70
4.3.6 Results 72
4.3.6.1 Manipulation and Realism Check 72
4.3.6.2 Construct Measurement 73
4.3.6.3 Hypothesis Testing 75
4.4 Study 2—Consequences of Rejections and the Role of the Number of Rejections 78
4.4.1 Study Objective 78
4.4.2 Study Design 79
4.4.3 Implementation 79
4.4.4 Recruitment and Composition of the Sample 80
4.4.5 Operationalization of Variables 80
4.4.6 Results 81
4.4.6.1 Manipulation and Reality Check 81

4.4.6.2 Construct Measurement 83
4.4.6.3 Hypothesis Testing 84
4.5 Study 3—Analysis of the Consequences of Rejections Using a Field Study 87
4.5.1 Study Objective 87
4.5.2 Study Design 88
4.5.3 Implementation 89
4.5.4 Recruitment and Composition of the Sample 92
4.5.5 Operationalization of Variables 94
4.5.6 Results 95
4.5.6.1 Construct Measurement 95
4.5.6.2 Propensity Score Matching 98
4.5.6.3 Difference-in-Differences Estimation 102
4.5.6.4 Hypothesis Testing 102
4.5.6.5 Post-hoc Analysis 105

5 Conclusion 111
5.1 Summary of Findings 111
5.2 Implications for Marketing Research and Practice 114
5.2.1 Implications for Marketing Research 114
5.2.2 Implications for Marketing Practice 115
5.3 Limitations and Directions for Future Research 117

References 119

List of Figures

Fig. 1.1	Structure of the research	5
Fig. 2.1	Process of a product test	8
Fig. 2.2	Effects of rejections in social psychology	24
Fig. 2.3	Effects of rejection in human resource management	26
Fig. 2.4	Effects of rejections in marketing	29
Fig. 2.5	Possible influencing factors on the perception of rejections in social psychology	31
Fig. 2.6	Possible influencing factors on the perception of rejections in human resource management	32
Fig. 2.7	Possible influencing factors on the perception of rejections in marketing	34
Fig. 3.1	Analysis process of the exploratory qualitative study	43
Fig. 3.2	Attribution process	50
Fig. 3.3	Attribution process following a rejection	55
Fig. 3.4	Summary of the hypothesized relationships	63
Fig. 4.1	Experimental design of scenario experiment 1	69
Fig. 4.2	Scenario description for Scenario Experiment 1	71
Fig. 4.3	Results of PROCESS Model 4, Scenario Experiment 1	75
Fig. 4.4	Results of PROCESS Model 7, Scenario Experiment 1	76
Fig. 4.5	Study design of scenario experiment 2	78
Fig. 4.6	Results of PROCESS Model 4, Scenario Experiment 2	83
Fig. 4.7	Results of PROCESS Model 4, Scenario Experiment 2 with dummy coding	85
Fig. 4.8	Study design of the field study	87
Fig. 4.9	Process of the field study	89
Fig. 4.10	Creation of the personal code	90

Fig. 4.11 Distribution of participants 93
Fig. 4.12 Identified matching variables of the field study 99
Fig. 4.13 Development of commitment among rejected applicants and non-applicants. 104
Fig. 4.14 Distribution of participants in the post-hoc analysis. 106

List of Tables

Table 2.1 Differences between online product tests and product sampling 11
Table 2.2 Effects of product samples 14
Table 2.3 Literature overview of online product tests 19
Table 3.1 Causal model according to Weiner (1979; 1985; 1986) 49
Table 3.2 Possible consequences of consistent behavior 53
Table 4.1 Operationalization scenario experiment 1 72
Table 4.2 Assessment of construct measurement scenario experiment 1 74
Table 4.3 Operationalization of scenario experiment 2 81
Table 4.4 Assessment of construct measurement scenario experiment 2 82
Table 4.5 Operationalization of the field study 94
Table 4.6 Validation of construct measurement in the field study 96
Table 4.7 Determinants of application: Pre- and post-treatment survey 100
Table 4.8 Means before and after matching 103
Table 4.9 Determinants of application pre-treatment survey 108
Table 4.10 Means before and after matching: Post-hoc analysis 109

1 Introduction

At the outset (**Sect. 1.1**), the relevance of the topic for marketing research and practice is highlighted. The objectives of the study and the resulting research questions are then presented (**Sect. 1.2**), before finally (**Sect. 1.3**) outlining the structure of the investigation.

1.1 Relevance of the Topic for Marketing Research and Practice

Online product testing programs—defined as a marketing tool in which consumers apply to receive a product free of charge or at a discounted price—have developed into an important marketing instrument in recent years. Their aim is to obtain feedback from consumers in the form of a feedback form or an online review. Product testers commit to testing the product and, after the test phase, providing feedback via a questionnaire or an online review. Product tests are often used for newly developed and as yet unreleased or recently launched products (Han/Zhang 2018, p. 139; Hu/Pei/Xie 2014, p. 9). The products offered may be either physical or digital (Han/Zhang 2018, p. 139; Nejad et al. 2015, p. 83), and may include both high- and low-priced test products (Garnefeld et al. 2021, p. 708). Product tests increase positive word-of-mouth (WOM) behavior (Chae et al. 2017, p. 89) and encourage product testers to invest more effort in writing their online reviews (Garnefeld et al. 2021, pp. 715 f.). In addition, marketing agencies advertise that 63% of testers purchase the test product after the product test, 97% of testers purchase one or more products from the company, and 50% of testers follow the company on social media (Staples-Otis 2022). Feedback in the form of compiled evaluation forms or online reviews is often published either

K. L. Küpper, *Negative and Positive Effects of Rejections in Online Product Testing Programs*, https://doi.org/10.1007/978-3-658-49277-9_1

by the tester themselves or by the company. This increases the awareness of a product, brand, and company (Yao et al. 2017, p. 599).

A typical online product testing program proceeds as follows: First, a company offers a product test online via its own website, its online community, or its social media channels. Providers of such product tests may include manufacturers themselves (e.g., Henkel, Phillips, Adidas, and Ehrmann), as well as retailers (e.g., dm-drogerie markt, REWE, and MediaMarkt). Some manufacturers also commission marketing agencies (e.g., Konsumgöttinnen, Toluna, and trnd) to conduct their product tests. In the next step, interested consumers apply to participate in the product test. The company selects the product testers and sends rejections to the remaining applicants. The product testers receive the test product at home and test it within a specified period. After the test phase, they complete an evaluation form and/or write an online review of the test product (Garnefeld et al. 2017, p. 704; Lu et al. 2018, pp. 77–86).

In practice, companies usually offer only a limited number of free test products, so not every applicant can be selected as a product tester. Instead, a typically large number of applicants receive a rejection from the company. This means they are not selected as product testers and therefore do not receive the free product. For example, Yao et al. (2017, pp. 599 f.) found that in a sample of 122 product tests conducted by a major e-commerce company in China, there were on average 1,670 applicants for only 29 test products. This implies an acceptance rate of just 1.7% (Yao et al. 2017, pp. 599 f.). Lu et al. (2017, p. 80) also found that out of 122,000 applicants, only about 3% were selected as product testers over the course of a year. Looking at the product tests on the website of dm-drogerie markt GmbH & Co. KG, it is apparent that on average only 300 people review the products (dm-drogerie markt 2023). With a registered community of over 736,000 members, if only 1% of registered members apply for an average of 300 test products, more than 7,000 applicants would still receive a rejection.

In principle, a rejection is a negative message received by individuals after they have expressed interest in something planned. This form of rejection can come from another person or from a company. Originally, a rejection is based on social exclusion, which people experience repeatedly throughout their lives. As a social species, humans perceive their existence as threatened when they are ignored, excluded, or rejected by another individual (Leary 2001, pp. 3 f.). Studies in social psychology have shown that such rejection can lead to both physical and psychological pain (Eisenberger/Lieberman/Williams 2003, p. 292). In interactions with companies, such a rejection may be sent, for example, in response to a job application. Studies in the field of human resource management confirm the expected negative consequences for companies that have to reject job applicants. After receiving a rejection, rejected applicants tend to avoid the company or spread negative WOM (Bauer et al. 1998, p. 900; Feinberg/Meoli-Stanton/Gable 1996, p. 70). In the marketing context, however, there are only a few studies that address the consequences of rejections. In this context, "stockouts" of products/services, the rejection of consumer ideas, and losing in a competition or sweepstakes have been examined as types of rejection. Studies on these forms, however, yield inconsistent results. Both, possible negative consequences, such as deterioration of the company's image or customer attrition (Ge/Messinger/Li 2009, pp. 284 f.; Fitzsimons 2000, p. 264; Ward/Hill/Gardner 1988, p. 139), and possible positive consequences, such as increased customer participation following a rejection (Fombelle/Bone/Lemon 2016, p. 685; Piezunka/Dahlander 2019, p. 521), have been identified.

Rejections in online product testing programs, however, have not yet been examined, and due to the inconsistent findings for similar forms of rejection in the marketing context, it remains unclear how rejections in online product testing programs affect rejected applicants. Furthermore, it is uncertain what consequences companies can expect when they reject applicants in the context of an online product testing program. It is possible that companies may face both negative and positive consequences. On the one hand, it can be assumed that after receiving a rejection, the applicant will try to understand the reason for it. Based on attribution theory, it is possible that the applicant will question the company's motives behind the product test and become skeptical. This skepticism may lead to negative consequences for the company, such as a decrease in purchase intention and an increase in the intention to spread negative WOM. On the other hand, the applicant has consciously decided to apply for the product test and has thus made an active commitment. It is possible that the rejected applicant feels an even stronger commitment after the rejection. This, in turn, may lead to counter-intuitive positive consequences for the company, such as an increase in purchase intention or a decrease in the intention to spread negative WOM.

Online product testing programs represent a relevant marketing tool (Yao et al. 2017, p. 599), for which there is, however, still little research literature. The consequences of rejections have also been scarcely studied in the marketing context and have not yet been considered in the context of online product testing programs. This research gap is to be addressed by the present study. Examining the consequences of online product testing programs can yield important insights for marketing research and practice. The body of research on online product testing programs and on rejections can be expanded, and recommendations for companies conducting product testing programs can be derived.

1.2 Objectives and Research Questions

Initial assumptions suggest that rejections in online product testing programs can lead to both negative and positive consequences for companies. Accordingly, the central research question of this study is: How does a rejection in an online product tester program affect the applicant who was not selected?

This overarching question can be divided into three sub-questions:

1. Which psychological mechanisms explain the effects of a rejection in an online product testing program? Are there both positive and negative mechanisms at work?
2. Under what conditions does the effect of a rejection in an online product testing program occur?
3. How does a rejection influence the future behavior of rejected applicants?

To answer the research questions, a combination of different research methods is employed. Based on an exploratory qualitative survey and two psychological theories, relevant hypotheses are derived for empirical testing. Since online product testing programs offer various products across different price categories and the number of previous applications per applicant varies, these factors are also taken into account in this study. The proposed relationships are then examined in two scenario-based experiments and a field study. The aim is to identify the psychological mechanisms and thereby understand the behavior of rejected applicants. Ultimately, the intention is to close the identified research gap by answering the research questions. On this basis, new insights for marketing research and practice are to be generated.

1.3 Structure of the Study

The study is organized into five chapters. Figure 1.1 provides an overview of the structure of the research.

Chapter 1 introduces the topic and outlines the objectives of the research. Section 1.1 highlights the relevance of the topic for marketing research and practice. The objectives of the paper and the resulting research questions are presented in Sect. 1.2, before the current Sect. 1.3 explains the structure of the research.

Chapter 2 covers the conceptual foundations. Section 2.1 defines the term *online product testing program* and distinguishes it from related concepts. In

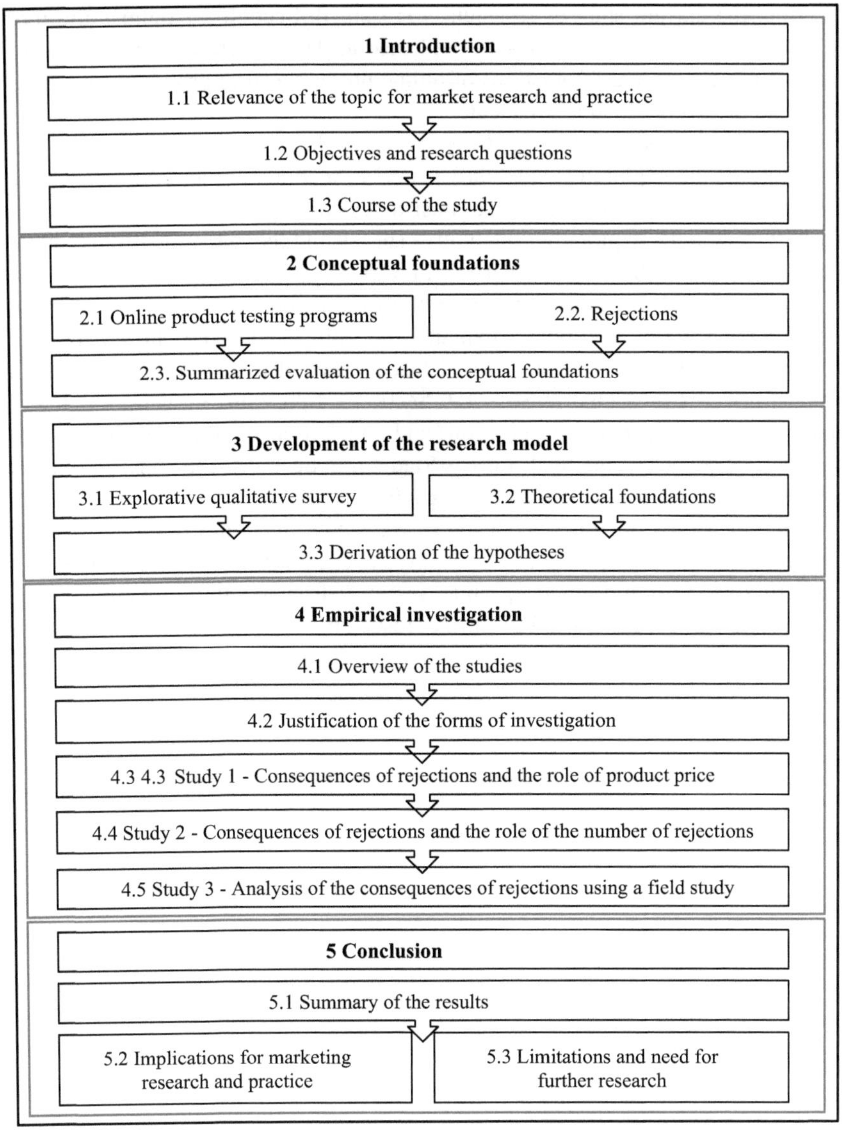

Fig. 1.1 Structure of the research. *(Source:* Own illustration)

addition, the current state of research is presented. Section 2.2 defines the term *rejection* and examines the research published to date in detail. Section 2.3 summarizes the conceptual foundations of online product testing programs and rejections and provides a final assessment.

Chapter 3 is dedicated to the development of the research model. Section 3.1 first presents the exploratory qualitative survey. Section 3.2 then introduces attribution theory and the commitment-consistency principle as theoretical foundations. Based on the exploratory qualitative survey and the theoretical foundations, the hypotheses for the study are derived in Sect. 3.3.

Chapter 4 addresses the empirical investigation. Section 4.1 provides an overview of the studies. Section 4.2 explains the rationale for the chosen research designs. Study 1, which examines the consequences of rejections and the role of product price, is presented in Sect. 4.3. Section 4.4 presents Study 2, which also analyzes the consequences of rejections and, in addition, examines the role of the number of rejections. The final study is Study 3. In Sect. 4.5, the consequences of rejections are once again examined using a field study.

Chapter 5 provides the conclusion of the study. Section 5.1 summarizes the findings and answers the research questions. Section 5.2 derives implications for marketing research and practice, while Sect. 5.3 discusses the limitations of the research and the resulting need for further research.

2 Conceptual Foundations

Within the chapter on conceptual foundations, the topics of online product testing programs (**Sect. 2.1**) and rejections (**Sect. 2.2**) are examined. The relevant terms are defined and conceptually distinguished from related concepts. In addition, an overview of the current state of research is provided for each of the two topics. The conceptual foundations of online product testing programs and rejections are summarized and evaluated (**Sect. 2.3**).

2.1 Online Product Testing Programs

The following section explains the fundamentals of online product testing programs. First, the term is defined (**Sect. 2.1.1**). Next, online product testing programs are differentiated from related concepts based on their characteristics (**Sect. 2.1.2**), and finally, an overview of the current state of research is provided (**Sect. 2.1.3**).

2.1.1 Definition of Terms

Online product tests are often conducted with new products, some of which are not yet available on the market (Cui et al. 2018, p. 1; Garnefeld et al. 2021, p. 703; Haenlein/Libai 2017, p. 71; Nejad/Amini/Babakus 2015, p. 68). The process of an online product testing program generally consists of seven steps, which are illustrated in Figure 2.1.

In the first step, **a company offers a test product**. This can take place, for example, on the company's own website, within its own community, or on its

K. L. Küpper, *Negative and Positive Effects of Rejections in Online Product Testing Programs*, https://doi.org/10.1007/978-3-658-49277-9_2

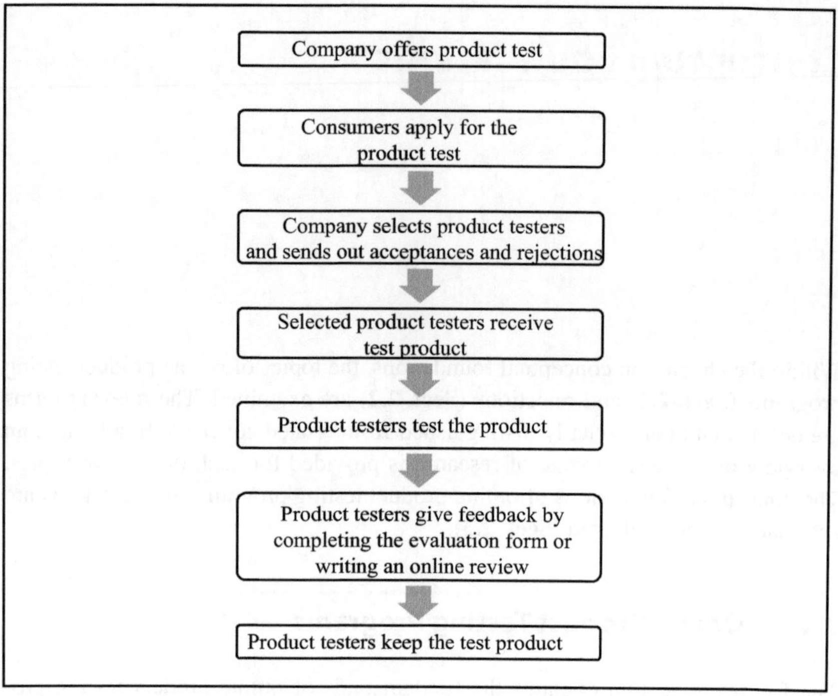

Fig. 2.1 Process of a product test. (*Source:* Own illustration)

social media channels. If the company already has a community dedicated exclusively to product testing, interested individuals can register at any time and will be notified as soon as they can apply for a new product test (e.g., dm-drogerie markt product tester community). Providers of such product tests may include manufacturers themselves, retailers, or agencies. Agencies often already have a large number of community members and can therefore reach the desired target group more quickly than manufacturers or retailers (Sautmann 2016, p. 177). Some agencies also specialize in certain product categories (e.g., Konsumgöttinnen for household goods). In general, newly developed products are often selected as test products in order to generate initial market awareness and obtain early product feedback (Yao et al. 2017, p. 599). The number of available test products varies greatly and depends on the product category and the price of the test product. For lower-priced test products, such as cosmetics or food items, several hundred test products are usually offered (REWE 2023, dm-drogerie markt 2023), whereas for high-priced electronics, only a few test products are typically made available (Phillips 2023, MediaMarkt 2023).

In the second step, **consumers can apply to participate in the product test**. Usually, only a few personal details and the address are requested. In some cases, providers wish to select product testers based on specific criteria and therefore ask for personal information such as hair type (dm-drogerie markt), household size ("Frag Team Clean"), or level of activity on social media (Phillips). This information is often collected once during registration for a product tester community. Companies want to ensure that the most relevant testers are selected and that these individuals will share their feedback within their social networks. Some companies also require applicants to write a kind of motivation letter with a predetermined word count, in which they must explain in writing why they are suitable as testers ("Frag Team Clean").

In the third step, **the company selects the product testers**. The selection can be based on the information provided in the application. This means that testers are specifically chosen from whom the company expects the most valuable feedback. This is also the usual selection principle for product tests conducted via marketing agencies. Another possibility is that the company uses a random draw to decide who will be selected as a product tester. Some companies do not disclose their selection process at all, leaving applicants to speculate about how testers are chosen (dm-drogerie markt 2023; MediaMarkt 2023; Lu et al. 2018, p. 77 f.). Companies generally send acceptance or rejection notifications to applicants by email. In some cases, the next product test is already promoted in this communication.

In the fourth step of the product test, **the selected testers receive their test product**. Usually, testers receive the product free of charge delivered to their home. However, there are also programs, such as those from REWE, in which the selected tester receives a voucher code that can be used to pick up the product free of charge at a physical store. This can be advantageous for the company, as the tester may make additional purchases in-store, creating cross-selling opportunities (Zhang/Go/Lin 2017, p. 4). At the same time, the company does not have to handle shipping the test products. If the test product is a digital product (e.g., a computer game or software), testers receive digital access.

In the fifth step, **the product testers test the product**. The testing period is determined by the company and usually lasts two to four weeks (Phillips, "Frag Team Clean"; MediaMarkt "Testpiloten"). During this period, product testers are expected to use the product in their daily lives, testing all its features and forming an opinion about it. In some cases, the company provides guidance on optimal use or instructions on how to document the testing process with photos and videos (Phillips 2023).

After the testing phase, in the sixth step, product testers must **provide their feedback**. In some cases, testers receive a link to an online questionnaire in which they must answer questions and also report freely on their experiences. This questionnaire may already be included as a paper form in the product packaging. In other cases, testers are required to share their feedback publicly on their social media channels or send it to the company, which then publishes the online reviews or photos and videos via its own channels (MediaMarkt 2023; REWE 2023).

After submitting feedback or publishing the material, the product test ends and the **product tester is allowed to keep the test product**. In a few exceptions, especially for more expensive test products (e.g., at Phillips, trnd) or if no review is submitted, the company reserves the right to reclaim the test product. In some programs, testers can also purchase the product from the company at a discounted price (trnd 2023; MediaMarkt 2023).

The following definition of a product test can be derived for the purposes of this research:

Online product tests are a marketing tool in which consumers apply electronically to a manufacturer, retailer, or agency to receive a product free of charge or at a discounted price. In return, product testers commit to thoroughly testing the product and, after the testing phase, providing feedback in the form of a questionnaire or an online review. This feedback is often published either by the tester themselves or by the company.

2.1.2 Differentiation from Related Concepts

Online product testing programs share certain components with other marketing activities. They are most similar to product sampling, which is why distinguishing between the two approaches is relevant for this study.

Jain, Mahajan, and Muller (1995, p. 125) define product samples as follows: "Samples are offers of free amount or trial of a product for consumers." In this case, the customer receives the product or a product sample free of charge. If the customer is to test a service instead, this is referred to as a "free trial" (free access).

Table 2.1 provides an overview of the characteristics of the measures and highlights the differences between them.

Table 2.1 Differences between online product tests and product sampling

Distinguishing Features	Online Product Tests	Product Sampling
Product	Complete product	Small product sample or limited access
Product Type	Not restricted	Primarily consumer goods
Participation Requirement	Active application by consumers	No requirements
Distribution	Targeted or random	Arbitrary or targeted to a consumer
Mode of Implementation	Online	Online and offline
Primary Objectives	Gathering feedback on new products; Increasing awareness of the product, brand, and company	Converting testers into customers; Increasing positive WOM in the form of online reviews
Participant Obligation	Obligation to provide feedback	No obligations

Source: Own illustration.

In contrast to most sampling campaigns, full-fledged **products** are provided to testers in a product test (Zhang/Go/Lin 2017, p. 5). In sampling, small product samples or, in the case of services, time-limited access is distributed. There are two common forms of distributing access to services. On the one hand, companies can provide time-limited access, which usually allows full use of the service. The other option is to distribute a demo version, where the consumer receives a version with limited functionality (Cheng/Liu 2012, p. 488). The **type of product** in online product tests is not restricted. Test products can be either consumer goods, such as toothpaste, or durable goods, such as electronics or books (Zhang/Go/Lin 2017, p. 5). In product sampling, primarily consumer goods are distributed (Sprott/Shimp 2004, p. 312; Yao et al. 2014, p. 1; Zhang/Go/Lin 2017, pp. 2 ff.). The **requirement for participation** in a product test is an active application by the consumer. In a product test, the test product is only distributed after a successful application. This means that the applicant must first complete an application and is then selected by the company as a tester (Yao et al. 2017, p. 599). In product sampling, on the other hand, participants do not have to meet any requirements.

The method of **distribution** also differs between the two measures. The selection of product testers within a product tester program can be targeted based on the information provided in the application or random through a lottery process.

The selected testers then receive the test product by mail (Zhang/Go/Lin 2017, p. 5). Distribution in product sampling differs from product testing, as it can take place through various channels: The product can be distributed by the company—via a promoter—either personally and directly or impersonally in the form of a coupon to the customer. In addition, the company must determine the location of distribution. The customer can be approached directly at the point of sale or at another public location. Delivery of the sample to the customer's home is also possible. If there is an option to attach a product sample to another product from the same company or to a magazine, there is a high likelihood that the customer will also test the product in this way (Gedenk 1999, pp. 91 f.; Jain/Mahajan/Muller 1995, p. 125).

The **implementation** of the entire product test—from the call for applications, through application and distribution, to feedback to the company—takes place online (Zhang/Go/Lin 2017, p. 3). In contrast, product sampling can be conducted both offline and online. Due to increasing digitalization and the spread of the internet, companies operating online are now also using product sampling as a marketing tool and offering samples. An example of this is the film streaming service Netflix, which provides consumers with free access to movies and series for a limited period. Conducting such an online campaign offers several advantages over the offline market. For example, it is easier for companies to reach a larger audience online. Offline, only those people who are present at the product sampling location are reached (Foubert/Gijsbrechts 2016, p. 810; Yao et al. 2017, p. 599).

The **primary objectives** of an online product testing program are to obtain feedback and increase awareness of a new product, brand, or company (Garnfelde et al. 2021, pp. 704 f.). Receiving feedback in the form of a completed questionnaire after the test phase and generating online reviews are essential for companies. Acquiring new customers is not the main focus, as many product testers frequently apply to various companies to receive free test products. Moreover, especially for durable goods such as cameras, it is unlikely that testers will purchase another camera shortly after the product test. The primary goal of product sampling campaigns, on the other hand, is to acquire new customers, particularly for newly developed products. For this reason, Yao et al. (2017, p. 599) define product sampling as an old but effective measure that companies can use to enter a new market, promote a new product, or increase sales of an existing product. These objectives can be achieved through product sampling by allowing customers to test the product and thus eliminate any uncertainties they may have about it. In doing so, they incur no risk of financial loss (Jain/Mahajan/Muller 1995, p. 125; Yao et al. 2017, p. 599). Another goal of product sampling is to increase positive WOM in the form of online reviews. By testing the product, the consumer is to be convinced and encouraged to share their experiences with other consumers (Haenlein/Libai 2017, p. 71). This goal can also be achieved in product sampling by specifically distributing samples to testers who are then expected to share their opinions with other consumers via social media or write online reviews on the provider's website (Chae et al. 2017, p. 89). Micro-influencers (influencers with a reach of between 1,000 and 100,000 followers) are often selected as testers to reach a large audience with the campaign. They primarily receive consumer goods such as food, household products, or cosmetics and health products to test. Testers are encouraged to publish their honest opinions and to disclose their participation in the campaign (Dost et al. 2019, p. 65).

Another important distinguishing feature is the **obligation** that participants in the campaigns undertake. In product testing, applicants commit to providing feedback to the company after the testing phase if their application is successful. Thus, completing a feedback form or writing an online review is mandatory for participants. Some companies reserve the right to reclaim the test product or exclude testers from future product tests if this obligation is not fulfilled (MediaMarkt 2023). In addition, in the case of an online review, it is usually specified on which website it must be published. As a result, product testers have no freedom in how they can provide their feedback. In contrast, with product sampling, consumers incur no obligations to the company upon receiving the product sample (Schlereth et al. 2013, p. 48). They are therefore not required to provide feedback or share information. Even explicitly selected testers are merely asked to share their opinion and, as a rule, receive only the test product itself as compensation, with no further payment (Dost et al. 2019, p. 65).

2.1.3 State of Research

Since online product testing programs have only recently been implemented, there is currently little research on this marketing tool. For this reason, the following section presents the current state of research on sampling and online product testing programs. First, the effects of samples or product trials are described (**Sect. 2.1.3.1**), followed by a discussion of the design features of a sampling campaign (**Sect. 2.1.3.2**), and finally, the researched effects of online product tests are explained (**Sect. 2.1.3.3**).

2.1.3.1 Mechanisms of Product Sampling

Part of the research on product sampling focuses on its effects on consumers. The temporal dimensions are divided into the moment of receipt and use of the sample, the immediate purchase process thereafter (short-term effect), and subsequent purchase processes (long-term effect). In her article, Gedenk (1999, p. 93) links these temporal dimensions to three measurement objects. She examines the effects of product samples on the tester's perception, attitude, and behavior. Table 2.2 illustrates the possible effects.

With successful **distribution of product samples** (the first temporal dimension), the consumer's **perception** is initially stimulated. The consumer recognizes the product sample and recalls the product. In the case of inefficient distribution (e.g., if the targeted consumers do not accept the sample), this perception does not occur, and thus neither short- nor long-term effects can arise. If the consumer finds the product attractive after use, their **attitude** changes, and they are highly likely to use the product. Receipt and use therefore influence the consumer's **behavior** (Gedenk 1999, p. 93).

Product samples are specifically used to achieve **short-term effects**, such as increasing product sales and, consequently, company sales (Chandukala et al. 2017 p. 504 f.; Chen et al. 2017 p. 89, Dost et al. 2019 p. 76, Zhou/Duan 2015, p. 21 f.). The evaluation of the product sample is followed by the evaluation of the product or company, based on the consumer's newly formed **attitude** (Baum et al. 2019, p. 95; Foubert/Gijsbrechts 2016, p. 810; Wang et al. 2013, p. 189). Product samples reduce consumer uncertainty through direct experience with the product. This allows testers to evaluate before purchase whether the product meets their needs (Cheng/Liu 2012, p. 493; Foubert/Gijsbrechts 2016, p. 820; Hu et al. 2010, p. 374 ff.; Wu/Deng/Jiang 2018, p. 192 f.). At the same time, distributing test products can be perceived as a signal of quality (Heiman et al. 2001, p. 533 f; Hu et al. 2010, p. 374 ff.; Smith/Swinyard 1983, p. 265 f.).

Table 2.2 Effects of product samples

		Temporal Dimensions of Effects		
		Distribution of Product Sample	Short-term Effect (first purchase after sample distribution)	Long-term Effect (subsequent purchase processes)
Substantive Dimensions of Effects	Perceptions	Ad Recall	–	–
	Attitudes	Evaluation of the Product Sample	Product Evaluation;Company Evaluation	Product Image; Company Image
	Behavior	Sample Usage	Product Sales; Company Sales	Brand Loyalty; Customer Loyalty

Source: Adapted from Gedenk 1999, p. 93.

Product samples generate greater trust than other forms of advertising, as customers can gain their own product experience. Exaggerated advertising can create high expectations among consumers, which may later lead to dissatisfaction if these expectations are not met. In contrast, this does not occur with the use of product samples. However, the careful use of advertising alongside a sampling campaign can also provide additional benefits, resulting in short- or long-term effects (Marks/Kamins 1988, p. 279). The sequence of actions within campaigns should be considered. If the sampling campaign is conducted before advertising, customer expectations of the product are not yet high. Subsequent advertising, however, has less influence on consumer behavior and attitude. If, on the other hand, advertising is launched first, the product is noticed by many people, many of whom may want to try it. However, this also carries the risk that expectations of the product will rise (Marks/Kamins 1988, p. 279). When products are tested at the point of sale and positively evaluated, this often leads to favorable **behavior** for the company, with the tester purchasing the product. Product and company sales increase. In addition, word-of-mouth (WOM) often spreads, leading to further sales growth. The increase in WOM can be attributed to the fact that consumers who receive a free product sample often wish to reciprocate and show their appreciation to the company (Baum et al. 2019 p. 95; Bond et al. 2019, p. 287 f.; Gedenk 1999, p. 94; Heiman et al. 2001, p. 533 f.; Chen/Duan/Zhou 2017, p. 83).

Bawa and Shoemaker (2004, p. 359 f.) identify three effects of sampling on product sales: acceleration effect, expansion effect, and cannibalization effect. The acceleration effect means that consumers begin to use the product earlier due to the product sample. The expansion effect leads to an enlargement of the target group, as people consume the product who had not originally intended to do so. However, sampling can also have a negative effect. Due to the free distribution of products, a cannibalization effect may occur, as the number of regular purchases is reduced because of the distribution. In both experiments conducted by Bawa and Shoemaker, however, the positive effects on sales outweighed the observed cannibalization effect (Bawa/Shoemaker 2004, p. 359 f.).

In addition to short-term effects, product samples can also have **long-term effects on subsequent purchase processes** (Bawa/Shoemaker 2004, p. 359 f.). In the long term, the **attitude** toward the product and the company can change, leading to brand loyalty or customer loyalty (Foubert/Gijsbrechts 2016, p. 810; Gedenk 1999, p. 94; Wu/Deng/Jiang 2018, p. 192 f.). Bettinger, Dawson, and Wales (1979, p. 35 ff.) also examined the long-term effects of product samples in their study. Their research showed that testing a product can create new acceptance. Products previously considered typical children's products can, when sampled by adults, acquire a new product image. This suggests that distributing product samples can lead to a **change in behavior** and thus to the acquisition of a new customer group (Bettinger/Dawson/Wales 1979, p. 35 ff.; Libai et al. 2013, p. 161). In general, offering product samples helps in the long term to change the image of the product and the provider, and can thus lead to brand or customer loyalty (Bawa/Shoemaker 2004, p. 345; Gedenk 1999, p. 106; Gedenk/Neslin 1999, p. 450 ff.).

2.1.3.2 Design Features of a Product Sampling Campaign

For the optimal planning of a sampling campaign, several design features must be determined. These include product selection, sampling size, the targeted consumers, and the timing of the program.

An important decision in designing a product sampling campaign is the **product selection**. A distinction can be made between the distribution of physical and digital products (Zhang/Goh/Lin 2017, p. 2). Chen, Duan, and Zhou (2017, pp. 82 ff.) investigated the effects of samples in their study and identified which products experience the greatest impact. They found that digital product samples lead to an increase in word-of-mouth, which in turn boosts sales. This effect is stronger for unknown products than for already established and well-known products. The cannibalization effect is low in the software market, whereas the number of online reviews increased by almost a third when the number of distributed accesses was doubled. Therefore, the authors recommend offering especially digital niche products and new products for testing. Product sampling draws attention to these products, provides consumers with information, and allows them to assess quality. The chances of being noticed in the market increase with sampling (Chen/Duan/Zhou 2017, pp. 82 ff.). In addition, the effort and costs of distributing digital products are lower than those for physical products (Chellappa/Shivendu 2005, p. 413; Gedenk 1999, p. 107; Nejad/Amini/Babakus 2015, p. 83). Wright and Lynch (1995, p. 716) found in their study that consumers preferred to test products with experience attributes, while traditional advertising was more effective for products with search attributes.

There are varying research findings regarding the optimal **sampling size**. Jain, Mahajan, and Muller (1995, p. 131) focused on new products prior to market entry. They examined the relationship between the quantity of product samples and economic indicators such as gross margin. According to their results, the optimal sampling size for durable goods is 5–7% of market potential. For consumer goods, however, the repurchase rate must be considered. If the product's repurchase rate is low, meaning few consumers will buy the product again in the near future, the sampling size should be greater than the repurchase rate. Only then will enough people be reached through distribution to generate a positive effect on sales figures. Since Jain, Mahajan, and Muller did not consider competition in their study and focused exclusively on new products before market entry, it is not surprising that there are further research findings on the optimal sampling size. Other authors therefore deviate from Jain, Mahajan, and Muller's recommendation and suggest a distribution rate of 0.2 to 1%, measured against the total size of the target group (Aral et al. 2013, p. 15; Nejad/Amini/Babakus 2015, p. 78).

Other studies examining the sampling process focus on the **targeted consumers**. Schlereth et al. (2013, pp. 63 f.) aimed in their study to identify suitable consumers as potential testers. Their analysis of the communication network as an information source for consumers shows that selecting the right testers has a greater impact on sales than the optimal sampling size. In addition, it is confirmed that the social network of the targeted customers plays an important role. If a company succeeds in finding consumers who are well connected socially (influencers), positive effects become apparent more quickly (Schlereth et al. 2013, pp. 63 f.). These influencers can reach a large number of people and usually have many followers who trust their opinions (Haenlein/Libai 2013, pp. 70 f.; Hinz et al. 2011, p. 68; Nejad/Amini/Babakus 2015, p. 81). When selecting targeted consumers, the approach can be either targeted or random. According to Haenlein and Libai (2013, pp. 70 f.), a targeted approach to customers considered the most profitable or best connected leads to the greatest success. In general, it can be stated that the selection of product testers and the number of targeted consumers depend on many factors, such as campaign costs, the product, and implementation (Groeger/Buttle 2014b, p. 1 188; Haenlein/Libai 2017, p. 86; Nejad/Amini/Babakus 2015, pp. 82 f.; Schlereth et al. 2013, pp. 60 ff.).

There are also varying research findings regarding the **timing** of a product sampling campaign. Companies must determine both the start date and the duration of the campaign. Foubert and Gijsbrechts (2016, pp. 810 ff.) studied the optimal timing for services and argue that it can only occur after an extensive test phase. One result of the study is that sampling initially leads to more customers starting to use the service. During use, consumers gain a much more detailed insight than through advertising. They directly perceive the quality of the service and are inclined to share their experiences as WOM with others. However, the quality of the test product has the greatest influence on the optimal timing of distribution. If the quality is still too low at the start of distribution, consumers will notice and spread negative WOM. This can result in potential customers deciding not to purchase the product, contrary to their original intention. Therefore, it is necessary to set the distribution date so that quality can be sufficiently tested in advance and good quality is ensured (Foubert/Gijsbrechts 2016, pp. 810 ff.).

Other researchers see the optimal distribution time as being as early as possible, even before market entry, in order to achieve the greatest possible effects (Han/Zhang 2018, p. 139; Hu et al. 2014, p. 9). Heiman et al. (2001) investigated the optimal timing for products already available on the market. A product sampling campaign can still be worthwhile even if the product is no longer new or is a niche product that has been available for some time. Since the product is already known to customers, the optimal distribution time changes. The authors found that even for mature products, distribution through sampling can still increase sales by counteracting product forgetting (Heiman et al. 2001, pp. 542 f.). In addition to the optimal timing of sampling, the duration of implementation must also be determined. Cheng and Liu (2012, p. 503) found in their study on the optimal duration that it depends on several factors. The functionality of the sample, consumer perception, and aggregate costs must be considered. Therefore, it is difficult to determine the duration in advance (Cheng/Liu 2012, p. 503).

2.1.3.3 Effects of Online Product Testing

Only a few studies have examined the effects of online product tests. Table 2.3 presents the studies along with the variables and effects investigated.

Studies published to date on online product tests focus on the positive effects of accepted testers. Yao et al. (2017, p. 609) show that online product tests can increase sales. The product testing program examined was published online on the company's website. During a one-week period, customers could apply to participate in the product test, and testers were selected. After the test phase ended, testers were asked to provide feedback. Yao and colleagues (2017, p. 609) found that, contrary to their expectations, online product testing programs with physical products were more beneficial for well-known brands than for lesser-known brands. Prior to the study, the authors assumed that online product testing programs would primarily help lesser-known brands by reducing customers' initial uncertainty about the unfamiliar brand. One possible reason for the success of well-known brands is that they attract more attention online and are more interesting to consumers. As a result, product tests for these brands are also more appealing to consumers, leading to a higher number of applicants. This finding is supported by the fact that companies with well-known brands observe both a direct and a long-term impact on sales. In contrast, lesser-known brands experience only a long-term effect from the online product testing program, which

Table 2.3 Literature overview of online product tests

Study	Variables/Contexts Investigated					Method	Effects of/on		Results
	Independent	Dependent	Mechanisms	Context Variables	Context		Accepted Testers	Rejected Testers	
Yao et al. (2017)	Product test	Sales	Product uncertainty Product quality	Brand awareness, Price, Product type, Number of products, Number of applicants	Various product types from an online retailer (including household, clothing, electronics)	Field study	**Positive effects** on sales through accepted testers		Online product tests were able to increase the sales of physical products. Well-known brands achieve greater benefits in terms of both immediate and later sales increases.
Zhang/Go/Lin (2017)	Type of test product	Sales of other products from the same seller Sales of the same test product from another seller		Product type	Test products from 100 categories on a product tester community site	Field study	**Positive effects** on sales through accepted testers, depending on product type		Product testing of a search good increases the sales volume of other products from the same seller. For experience goods, there are cross-store spillover effects that increase the sales of the same product from another seller.

(continued)

Table 2.3 (continued)

Study	Variables/Contexts Investigated					Method	Effects of/on		Results
	Independent	Dependent	Mechanisms	Context Variables	Context		Accepted Testers	Rejected Testers	
Garnefeld et al. (2021)	Acceptance of product testers	Review rating Review quality	Inequality Pressure	Price, Product complexity, Number of reviews	Physical products from 13 categories (including books, electronics, toys)	Qualitative interviews, experiments, field study	**Positive effects** on review rating and quality of accepted testers depending on price, number, and complexity		Product tests increase review ratings under certain conditions.

Source: Own illustration.

is nevertheless significantly stronger for well-known brands. In summary, staging an online product testing program with an application phase for well-known brands has a pronounced advertising effect, allowing companies to benefit both in the short and long term (Yao et al. 2017, p. 609).

Zhang, Go, and Lin (2017, pp. 1 ff.) also focus on the positive effects of accepted testers on sales. In their study, they used field data from the largest online product testing agency in China and analyzed product tests from 254 manufacturers and retailers in around 100 different product categories. Testers could apply for individual product tests and, after successful application, test the product free of charge. The completed reviews were then published on the respective websites of the manufacturers and retailers. Analysis of the individual product categories revealed that the increase in sales depends on the type of product. Product tests of search goods increase the sales volume of other products from the same seller. For experience goods, there are cross-store spillover effects that increase the sales of the same product from another seller. Depending on their objectives, companies should therefore consider which products to offer as test products (Zhang/Go/Lin 2017, pp. 1 ff.).

Garnefeld et al. (2021, pp. 716 f.) examine the effects of accepted testers in online product testing programs on the submission of online reviews. Since product testing programs require testers to provide feedback, such as a review, in exchange for participation, product tests are an effective method for increasing the number of online reviews. The authors analyzed, among other things, 200,000 online reviews from product testers and found that testers do not automatically write higher-quality reviews or online reviews with higher star ratings. Instead, the effect of online product testing programs on online review quality and ratings depends on the price of the test product, product complexity, and the number of existing online reviews. Product testers write more positive online reviews for higher-priced test products that already have many published reviews. If a test product is both high-priced and complex, the reviews from product testers are of higher quality. However, if many online reviews have already been published for a product, testers invest less effort, resulting in lower online review quality. Thus, it was confirmed that product testing programs lead to an increase in the number of online reviews and, taking into account the price of the test product, product complexity, and the number of existing reviews, can also improve online review quality (Garnefeld et al. 2021, pp. 716 f).

The current state of research already reveals a research gap: Due to the novelty of this marketing tool, there is limited research on online product testing programs. To date, the focus has been on the positive effects of accepted testers in online product testing programs, while the potential effects on rejected applicants have not been investigated. Furthermore, existing studies have concentrated on the positive effects, neglecting possible negative effects for companies.

2.2 Rejections

The following section explains the fundamentals of rejections. First, the term is defined (**Sect. 2.2.1**), followed by an overview of the current state of research (**Sect. 2.2.2**).

2.2.1 Definition of Terms

A rejection is based on the social experience of being excluded, which a person may encounter. As a social species, humans perceive their existence as threatened when they are ignored, excluded, or ostracized by another individual (Leary 2001, pp. 3 f.). Defining rejection in social psychology is challenging for two reasons: First, contrasting acceptance and rejection leads to a dichotomous perspective, even though, at least in interpersonal relationships, there are clear gradations of acceptance and rejection. Second, individuals may quickly perceive a certain type of rejection, even if this was not intended by the other party (Leary/Twenge/Quinlivan 2006, p. 112). Leary (2001, pp. 4 ff.) therefore proposes a continuum with gradations and defines rejection as "status of low relational evaluation in which a person does not regard his or her relationship with another individual as valuable, important, or close."

In the context of a person's relationship with a company, rejection is usually unambiguous, as it is delivered in writing or communicated by an employee, and does not require clarification through various gradations. For example, a person may receive a clear rejection from a company after applying for something. This can occur in various situations, such as applying for a job position, entering a competition, or even in everyday attempts to purchase a product or service. A company may also send a written rejection to applicants as part of a product testing program.

In summary, the following definition of rejection can be derived for the purposes of this work:

A rejection is a negative response received after a person has expressed interest in something planned. This form of rejection can come from either another individual or a company.

2.2.2 State of Research

Rejections have so far been studied in three disciplines: social psychology, human resource management, and marketing. First, the effects of rejections in these three disciplines are described (**Sect. 2.2.2.1**), followed by an examination of the factors influencing the perception of rejections in these disciplines (**Sect. 2.2.2.2**).

2.2.2.1 Effects of Rejections

Rejections are widespread in everyday life, even though humans, as a social species, have an evolutionarily rooted aversion to rejection (Leary 2001, pp. 3 f.). **Social psychological** basic research has primarily addressed the questions of what constitutes interpersonal rejection and what effects rejection has on the rejected individual (Leary 2001; Williams/Zadro 2001). The majority of these studies focus on the relationship between two individuals. Within the research, the consequences of rejection in the relationship between an individual and a company are mainly considered in the context of **human resource management**. However, the findings on rejections in this academic discipline can only be partially transferred to the marketing context. There are only a few studies on rejections in the **marketing context,** and none that analyze rejections in product testing programs.

The effects of rejection and exclusion in interpersonal relationships have already been extensively studied in **social psychology**. Social psychology mainly analyzes the internal states following so-called "social exclusion" or "ostracism" (Leary 2001, pp. 5 f.). Ostracism is the extreme form of rejection. In this case, a person deliberately refuses contact with another person (e.g., when someone is asked to leave an event or is expelled from an organization). Social exclusion, as a less extreme form, is characterized by a person being ignored and interactions being avoided, while the other's presence is still tolerated (Leary 2001, pp. 5 f.; Wesselmann/Williams 2017, p. 694). A rejection in an interpersonal relationship mainly has negative consequences for the rejected individual. However, there are also a few positive effects that can occur after a rejection. Figure 2.2 provides an overview of the possible effects.

The deliberate exclusion of a person (ostracism) or ignoring a person (social exclusion) leads to the violation of four fundamental social needs: first, the need for belonging; second, the need for control; third, the need for recognition; and fourth, the need for high self-esteem. The need for belonging is evolutionarily determined. Only through belonging to a group were humans able to survive and ensure their continued existence (Ainsworth 1989, p. 709; Baumeister/Leary,

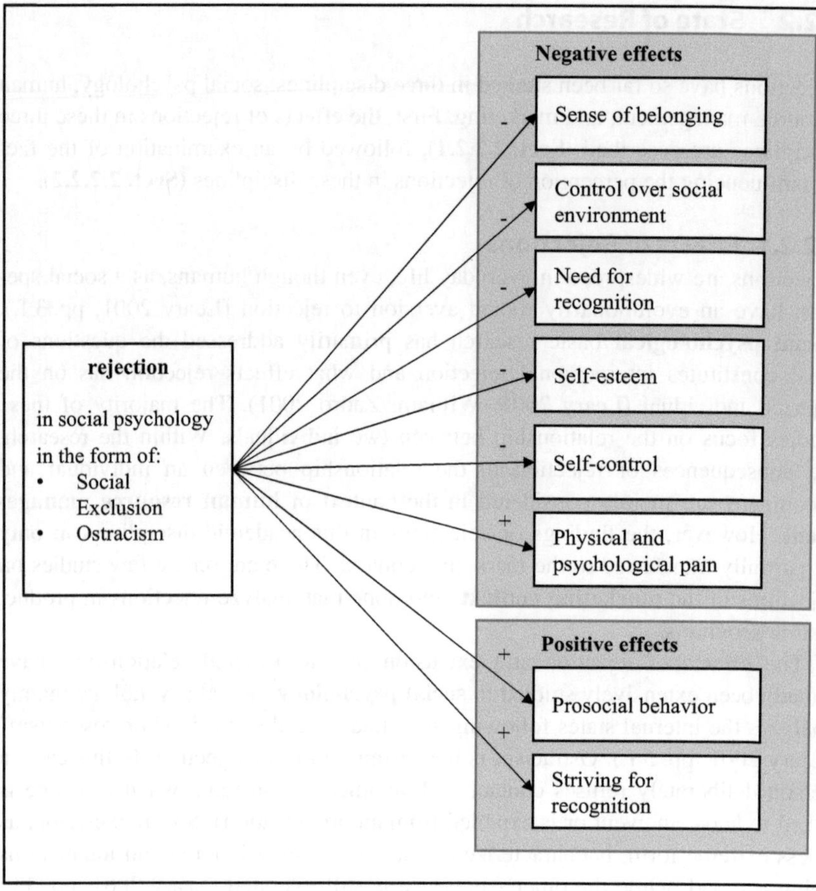

Fig. 2.2 Effects of rejections in social psychology. (*Source:* Own illustration)

1995, p. 499). Thus, people have a strong need for acceptance and social relationships, which is threatened by rejection (Leary 2001, pp. 3 f.; Wesselmann/Williams 2017, p. 694). A rejection leads to a reduction in the sense of belonging (Adler 1930, pp. 5 ff.; Baumeister/Leary 1995, pp. 502 f.; Williams/Zadro 2001, p. 48). At the same time, Williams and colleagues (2001, pp. 34 ff.) have demonstrated in several studies that rejection can reduce the feeling of control over one's social environment. It is important for individuals to understand their environment and to be able to influence others (Wesselmann/Williams 2017, p. 694; Burger, 1992, p. 7; Peterson/Seligman 1984, pp. 369 ff.).

Furthermore, a rejection disregards the need for recognition and diminishes self-esteem. This is because a rejection is associated with a form of punishment. It is accompanied by the implicit accusation that the individual has done something wrong (Williams 2001, p. 61). Criticism is therefore also quickly perceived as rejection and reduces self-esteem (Leary/Twenge/Quinlivan 2006, p. 125). In addition, rejection leads to a decrease in self-control. A rejected person has fewer cognitive resources to reflect on their actions and tends to act impulsively (Muraven/Tice/Baumeister 1998, pp. 786 f.; Leary/Twenge/Quinlivan 2006, p. 128). All these effects are accompanied by negative emotions such as sadness, anxiety, anger, or rage (Williams/Zadro 2001, pp. 30 f.). These emotions can trigger psychological pain in the individual, which closely resembles physical pain (Eisenberger/Lieberman/Williams 2003, p. 292).

However, there are also a few positive effects of rejection. Rejection can lead to an increase in prosocial behavior, meaning that individuals act in accordance with social expectations in order to be accepted by others. These efforts to gain recognition are undertaken to restore a sense of belonging to the group (Baumeister/Leary 1995, p. 502; Leary/Twenge/Quinlivan 2006, p. 112; Williams/Zadro 2001, pp. 48 f.). Individuals may, for example, become more involved in group work (Williams/Sommer 1997, p. 702) or actively seek to strengthen a relationship (Gonzaga et al. 2001, pp. 258 f.; Williams/Zadro 2001, pp. 48 f.).

The majority of the business management literature on rejection focuses on **human resource management** and analyzes rejection in the context of job applications. Personnel selection is a standardized process in which rejections are issued by the company and, ideally, are based on the applicants' skills and personality traits. In this field as well, both primarily negative and some positive effects can be observed. Figure 2.3 provides an overview of the possible effects of rejection in human resource management.

Particularly important aspects that ultimately determine how rejection affects human resource management are the perceived fairness and organizational justice towards the rejected applicant (Ambrose/Cropanzano 2003, p. 272; Bauer et al. 1998, p. 900; Gilliland 1993, p. 728; Walker et al. 2015, p. 999). According to Gilliland (1993, p. 716), the consequences of a rejection strongly depend on the applicant's expectations. A rejection can reduce perceived fairness if the applicant believes they possess the required skills and personality for the position but are still rejected. In particular, the procedural fairness perceived by the rejected applicant, as part of overall fairness, plays a role, as it influences whether

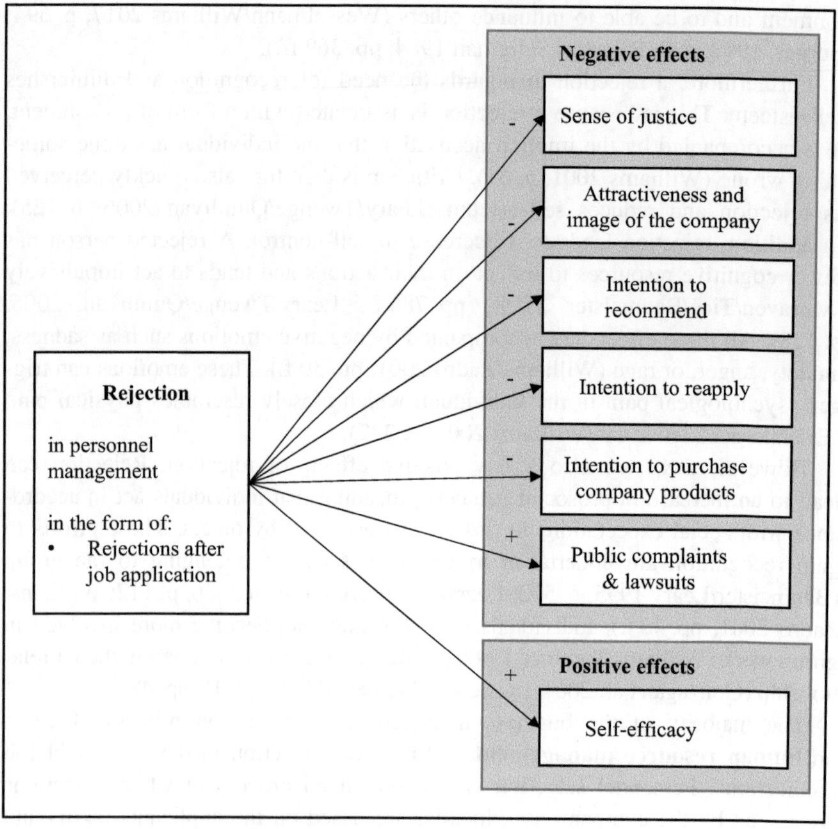

Fig. 2.3 Effects of rejection in human resource management. (*Source:* Own illustration)

the applicant attributes the rejection to themselves or to the company (Gilliland 1993, pp. 698 f.; Horvath/Ryan/Stierwart 2000, pp. 325 f.; Ployhart/Ryan 1997, pp. 327 f.). If a rejected applicant blames the company for the rejection, this can have negative consequences for the company, such as reduced attractiveness and a poorer image (Bauer et al. 1998, p. 900; Feinberg/Meoli-Stanton/Gable 1996, p. 70; Smither et al. 1993, p. 72).

Rejected applicants evaluate the company and the selection process less positively (Bauer et al. 1998, p. 900). In addition, rejected applicants show a lower willingness to recommend the company to others (Gilliland 1993, pp. 698 f.; Smither et al. 1993, p. 72; Ployhart/Ryan 1997, pp. 327 f.) and are also less likely to contact the company again or reapply (Feinberg/Meoli-Stanton/Gable 1996, p. 70; Hausknecht/Day/Thomas 2004, p. 640). Furthermore, it is possible that rejected applicants avoid contact with the company altogether, which can also reduce their intention to purchase the company's products (Hausknecht/Day/Thomas 2004, p. 640; Macan et al. 1994, p. 733). Smither and colleagues (1993, pp. 70 ff.) point out that public complaints may increase if a company issues a rejection that is clearly unjustified or based on an unfair selection process. In some serious cases, rejected applicants are even willing to pursue legal action (Smither et al. 1993, pp. 70 ff.).

If, on the other hand, a company succeeds in designing a fair selection process, rejection can have a positive influence on the behavior of rejected applicants. In this case, the rejected applicant attributes the rejection to themselves rather than to the company, and their self-efficacy can be enhanced. A fair selection process can be achieved, for example, if the company provides the applicant with constructive feedback and adequately assesses their performance (Gilliland 1993, p. 725; Bauer et al. 1998, p. 900; Müller/Moser 2006, p. 352; Ployhart/Ryan 1997, p. 331).

Rejection in **marketing** has so far been studied in three forms: First, **stockouts**, the unavailability or denial of products, and, analogously in the service sector, the denial of services; second, the **rejection of consumer ideas** in the context of co-creation; and third, **losing in a competition or game**. The most obvious and frequent rejection situation in the marketing context occurs when consumers are denied access to a product or service. **Stockouts**—when a physical product is not available in the desired form, flavor, or size, is not in saleable condition, or is not available at the expected location (Sanchez-Ruiz/Blanco/Kyguoliené, 2018, p. 103)—are a common phenomenon. In such cases, the applicant receives a rejection that is not directed at them personally but is simply justified by the lack of availability, or the company may select, for example based on customer status, which consumer will still receive a product or service in the event of scarcity. Consumer reactions to scarcity have been extensively analyzed (Ge/Messinger/Li 2009, pp. 274 ff.; Wangenheim/Bayón 2007, pp. 36 ff.; Helm/Hegenbart/Endres 2013, pp. 223 ff.).

Another situation in the marketing context in which rejections are issued is the **rejection of personal ideas** in the context of co-creation. The sharing of ideas by consumers is a marketing tool used by many companies. Consumers provide companies with ideas to improve their products or services. The likelihood of having one's idea rejected by a company is very high, at a rate of 98% (Fombelle/Bone/Lemon 2016, p. 685). Due to this high rate, applicants' expectations are generally low; however, the negative consequences are all the more pronounced, as the rejection is again perceived as personal and directed at the applicant and their idea, and the applicant clearly attributes the reason for the rejection to themselves.

A third situation in which rejections occur involves **competitions or prize draws** organized by companies, where typically not all consumers can win (Kalra/Shi 2010, p. 287). Most consumers who participate in prize draws lose and receive an (implicit) rejection. Compared to idea competitions, entering a prize draw is usually much quicker, and applicants do not invest much time or effort in their entry. Often, only contact details need to be provided, making it clear to the rejected applicant that the reason for the rejection is not personal, but simply a matter of bad luck in the drawing. Both primarily negative and occasional positive effects can be observed in the marketing context. In this dimension, both person-related and company-related effects can be identified. Figure 2.4 provides an overview of the possible effects of rejections in marketing.

In their study, Helm, Hegenbart, and Endres (2013, p. 239) summarize the extensive research on stockouts by analyzing the five most frequently studied consumer reactions to stockouts (switching stores, postponing or abandoning the purchase process, switching products, switching brands) in greater detail. Most consumers switch stores when a product is out of stock (41.5%), others postpone the purchase to a later date (22%), choose a different product (18.1%), abandon the purchase entirely (12.2%), or switch brands (6.3%). If the company manages to retain the customer despite the postponed purchase or the choice of a different product, no negative consequences arise for the company. However, if the customer leaves by abandoning the purchase completely or switching brands, the rejection results in negative effects for the company due to lost revenue (Helm/Hegenbart/Endres 2013, p. 239). For the company, customer rejection can also have positive effects, as a stockout can create a sense of urgency in the customer and increase the product's attractiveness (Ge/Messinger/Li 2009, pp. 284 f.). For consumers, stockouts are usually an unpleasant situation that forces them to make a quick decision, which can lead to dissatisfaction. However, if a stockout simplifies the decision-making process for the customer by reducing the number of available products, it can also have positive effects for the individual. This can lead to an increase in customer satisfaction (Fitzsimons 2000, p. 264).

The limited number of studies on the rejection of consumer ideas shows that consumers may respond to a rejected idea with diminished self-esteem and, consequently, a reduction in future participation (Fombelle/Bone/Lemon 2016, p. 685; Piezunka/Dahlander 2019, p. 521). Fombelle and colleagues (2016, p. 686) demonstrate that the rejection of a consumer idea reduces future participation by 59%. This can be explained by the fact that the rejection of a consumer idea, due to the

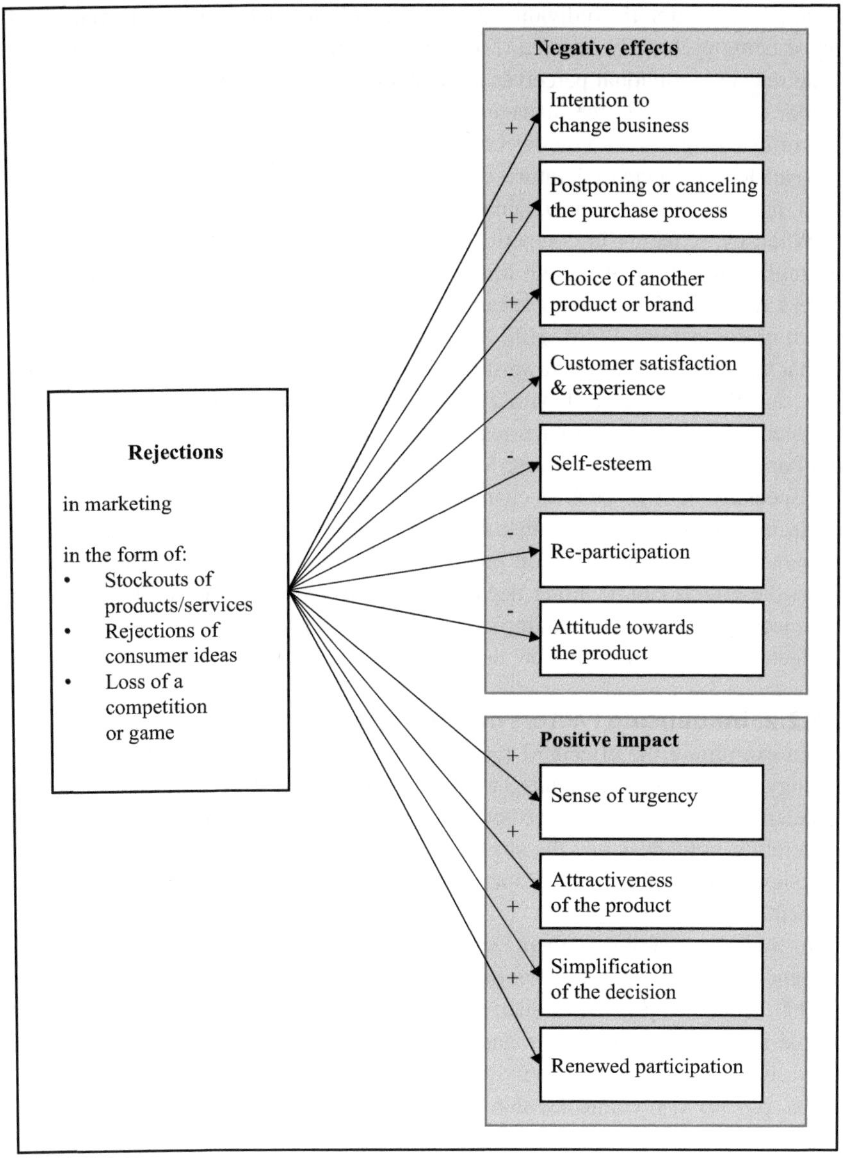

Fig. 2.4 Effects of rejections in marketing. (*Source:* Own illustration)

personal connection the individual has to their submitted idea, gives them the feeling of being personally rejected (Fombelle/Bone/Lemon 2016, p. 686). However, if the rejected individual perceives the rejection as appreciative, the rejection can, similar to human resource management, be interpreted as a form of feedback. If the company signals with the rejection that it is interested in further collaboration, this can lead to increased future customer participation (Fombelle/Bone/Lemon 2016, pp. 686, 701; Piezunka/Dahlander 2019, p. 521).

When participating in competitions and prize draws, applicants often receive an implicit rejection. Although this is not explicitly stated, the person is nevertheless rejected. This type of rejection can have negative consequences for the rejecting companies. Ward, Hill, and Gardner (1988, p. 139) found that losers have a less positive attitude toward the promoted product and the game than winners, and the likelihood of participation decreases after a rejection (Ward/Hill/Gardner 1988, p. 139). Another negative effect identified by Leclercq, Hammedi, and Poncin (2018, p. 93) is a deterioration in the customer experience.

Especially in cases such as changes in self-efficacy and self-esteem following a rejection, it becomes clear that the effects depend on moderators such as the implementation of the selection process or the communication of the rejection. Thus, the effects can be either negative or positive for the rejected individual or the rejecting company, depending on the situation. For this reason, these influencing factors are examined in more detail in Sect. 2.2.2.2.

2.2.2.2 Influencing Factors on the Impact of Rejections

When examining the effects of rejections in the three disciplines of social psychology, human resource management, and marketing, it becomes apparent that some effects can be assessed as both negative and positive. This is partly because moderating influences may be at play in these situations. Figure 2.5 provides an overview of the influencing factors studied regarding the perception of rejection in social psychology.

In social psychology, there are two opposing perspectives regarding the influencing factors of rejections on perception. McDonald and Donellan (2012, p. 617) fundamentally argue that in cases of extreme rejection (ostracism), all people react almost identically and that the negative effects of severe rejection are resistant to moderating individual differences. Williams, Cheung, and Choi (2000, p. 759) also confirmed that in cases of strong rejection, personal or situational factors have no influence. Other authors hold the view that personality variables such as gender, feelings of loneliness, need for belonging, and social anxiety should also not be considered as moderators (Williams/Cheung/Choi 2000, p. 759; Wirth/Lynam/Williams 2010, p. 400).

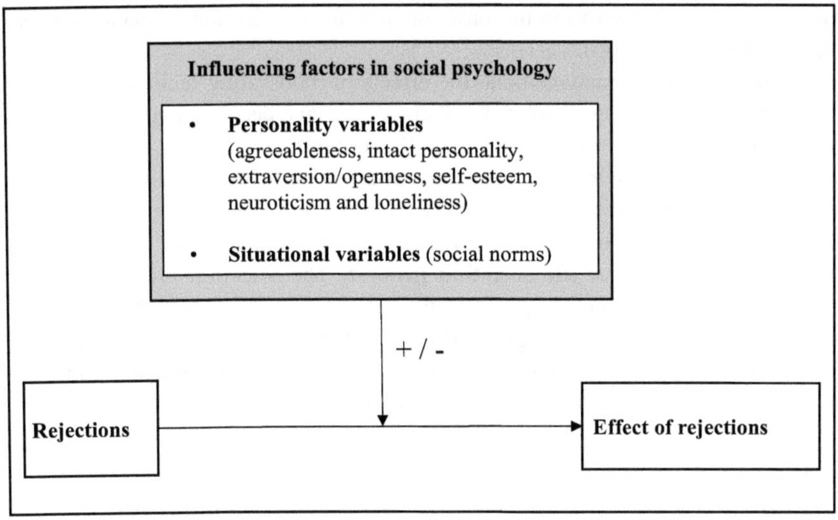

Fig. 2.5 Possible influencing factors on the perception of rejections in social psychology. (*Source:* Own illustration)

At the same time, some studies confirm the influence of **personality variables** on perception. McDonald and Donnellan (2012, p. 617) show that individuals with low levels of empathy are less affected by social exclusion. Wirth, Lynam, and Williams (2010, p. 400) examined various personalities in more detail and found that individuals with severe personality disorders are less affected by rejection than those with intact personalities. The confirmed association with disordered personality involved individuals with paranoia and schizophrenia. Empathy and extraversion were again confirmed as possible influencing factors that can mitigate the negative effects of rejection.

Another personality variable that influences the perception of rejection is self-esteem. Individuals with low self-esteem react more quickly to rejection than those with high self-esteem. The pain resulting from rejection is therefore worse for people with low self-esteem (Wirth/Lynam/Williams 2010, p. 400; Onoda et al. 2010, p. 389). Neurotic, lonely individuals also react particularly strongly on an emotional level to rejection (Boyes/French 2009, p. 397; Wesselmann et al. 2012, pp. 585 f). Rudert and Greifeneder (2016, p. 966) offer a new approach, examining the **situation** in which a person is rejected, and confirm social norms as a moderating influence on perception. A social norm helps the rejected individual determine the basis on which the rejection is made (Rudert/Greifeneder 2016, p. 966).

In human resource management, the effects of moderating factors can also be dependent. Figure 2.6 summarizes the factors that have been studied.

In human resource management, Gilliland (1993, p. 700 ff.) examines the reactions of applicants in a job selection process. He investigates both accepted and rejected applicants and incorporates various factors influencing the perception of a rejection into his model. Of particular importance are the correct implementation and **design of the selection process**. The selection process must be consistent and transparent in order to be perceived as fair. After the selection process is completed, the **design of the rejection** is also of great significance. A rejection should be formulated as appreciative feedback, and no important information should be withheld from the applicant. This view is also supported

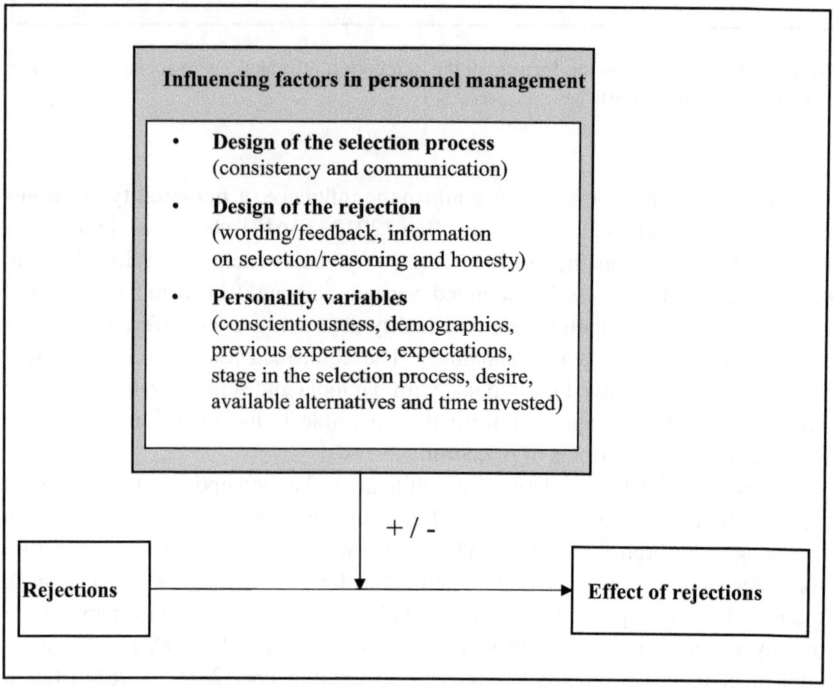

Fig. 2.6 Possible influencing factors on the perception of rejections in human resource management. *(Source:* Own illustration)

by Feinberg, Meoli-Stanton, and Gable (1996, p. 63). The wording of the rejection directly influences the company's image, the applicant's self-esteem, and future applicant behavior. If, in addition, the company provides information about the reasons for the rejection in an appropriate and honest manner, the rejection is perceived more positively than a standard response. Appropriate explanations in rejection letters can, for example, reduce feelings of unfairness and mitigate negative emotions toward the rejecting company (Feinberg/Meoli-Stanton/Gable 1996, p. 70; Gilliland et al. 2001, p. 698; Horvath/Ryan/Stierwalt 2000, p. 325 f.; Shapiro/Buttner/Barry 1994, p. 365 f.).

Hausknecht, Day, and Thomas (2004, p. 642) summarize, among others, the extensive studies by Gilliland (1993, p. 694 ff.) and Ryan and Ployhart (2000, p. 565 ff.) in their meta-analysis and develop an updated model of applicant reactions in the job selection process. In this model, **personality variables** are additionally listed as moderators. In addition to personality traits such as conscientiousness, age, gender, and ethnic background are also relevant. Previous experiences and the expectations an applicant has also play a decisive role in the perception of a rejection. Furthermore, the stage in the selection process last reached by the applicant, the desire for the position, and the available job alternatives are highly relevant (Hausknecht/Day/Thomas 2014, p. 642). Another personal factor influencing the perception of rejection is the time invested by the applicant. According to Rafaeli (1999, p. 710), the time invested is a predictor of an applicant's reaction, and especially the passive time during which the applicant can do nothing but wait can have a negative effect (Rafaeli 1999, p. 710).

The influencing factors on the effect of rejections in the marketing context are summarized in Fig. 2.7.

In **marketing**, most influencing factors relate to product stockouts, as this is the most extensively researched form of rejection in marketing. An overview is provided by the study of Helm, Hegenbart, and Endres (2013, p. 228), whose research model already lists a variety of influencing factors. Among the **personality variables**, demographics, purchasing behavior (whether hedonic or utilitarian in nature), acceptance of alternatives, as well as mobility and impulsiveness play a decisive role in the perception of stockouts. The **situational** factors influencing perception include the urgency of the purchase and the time available to the individual. If urgency is high and available time is low, the person tends to postpone or abandon the purchase. However, if the rejected individual demonstrates high loyalty (**company variable**) toward the company, the rejection is not perceived as severe, and the person merely switches products or purchases at a later time (Helm/Hegenbart/Endres 2013, p. 228). Fitzsimons (2000, p. 264) also confirms that personal attitude, the availability of alternatives, and

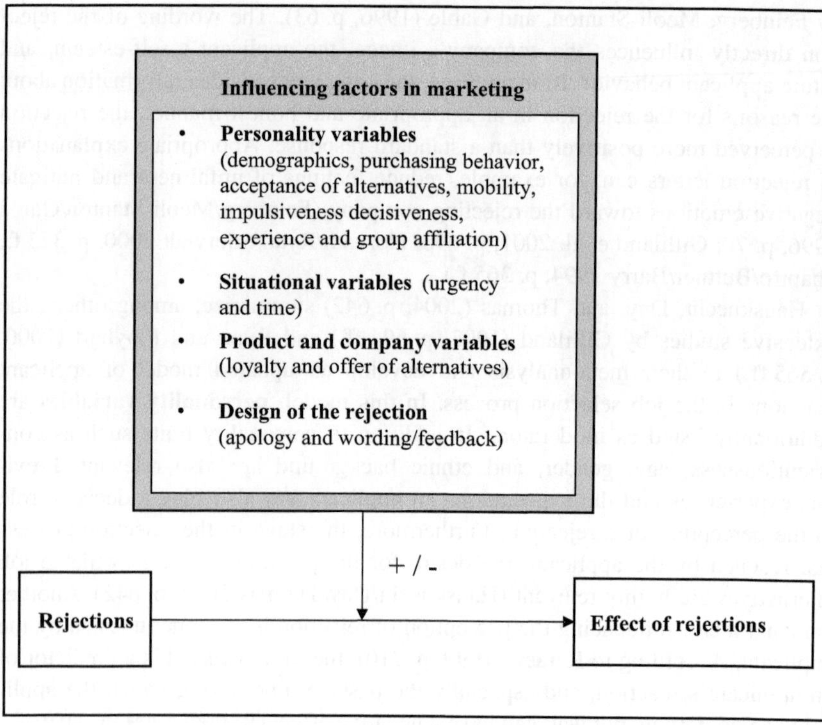

Fig. 2.7 Possible influencing factors on the perception of rejections in marketing. *(Source:* Own illustration)

the individual's decision-making difficulties influence whether the rejection is perceived as positive or negative. If the stockout makes the decision easier for the person and they also have a positive attitude toward the alternatives, the rejection may even be perceived as positive (Fitzsimons 2000, p. 264).

For the rejection of submitted consumer ideas, there are three additional factors influencing perception: previous experiences, perceived group membership, and the offering of an apology. If a consumer has already received a rejection from the company, this affects the perception of a subsequent rejection. However, if the company succeeds in establishing a strong sense of group membership among all applicants, the rejected individual perceives their own rejection as less negative. If the company also offers an apology for the negative response, the rejected applicant perceives the rejection as less severe, and the intention to participate in the future increases (Fombelle/Sterling/Lemon 2016, p. 701). As in human resource management, in the co-creation context the **design of the rejection** can be implemented in such a way that the rejected applicant perceives it as feedback. If the linguistic style of the rejection matches the submitted idea, the likelihood is highest that the applicant will view the rejection as a form of feedback rather than a mere rejection letter (Piezunka/Dahlander 2019, p. 521). In the perception of losses in competitions or sweepstakes, **personal** and demographic variables, but above all the previous experiences of the rejected individual, are important influencing factors (Ward/Hill 1991, p. 70; Leclercq/Hammedi/Poncin 2018, p. 93).

The current state of research reveals a research gap: rejections have so far been studied in three disciplines (social psychology, human resource management, and marketing). In social psychology, there is extensive research on the effects of interpersonal rejection. In human resource management, the effects of rejections and influencing factors have also been thoroughly investigated. In the marketing context, numerous studies exist only on rejections in the form of stockouts. There is far less research on the rejection of consumer ideas or in competitions and games, which, due to their similarity in terms of dimension and characteristics, most closely resemble rejections in online product testing programs. Therefore, it remains questionable to what extent these findings can be transferred to online product testing programs.

2.3 Summary Assessment of the Conceptual Foundations

Online product testing programs are still a relatively new marketing tool. What is distinctive about them is that companies distribute test products free of charge or at a discount to product testers after they have applied online. As part of the application process, consumers must provide their personal data and, in some cases, specific information about themselves or their household, or even submit a kind of motivation letter in certain programs. The company selects the testers and sends out the test products. These are not product samples, but full-sized products that testers are allowed to keep after the product test. In return, they commit to providing feedback to the company in the form of a completed questionnaire or an online review. Thus, online product testing programs differ from product sampling campaigns, particularly in their implementation, the completeness of the product, and the obligations undertaken by the applicants.

Previous research has focused primarily on product sampling. In this field, the positive impact dimensions have already been extensively studied, and the design features for optimizing such campaigns have been thoroughly examined. Only a few studies address online product testing programs (Garnefeld et al. 2021; Yao et al. 2017; Zhang/Go/Lin 2017). The very limited research in this area, in turn, focuses exclusively on the positive effects of these programs for companies. Moreover, these studies consider only the accepted product testers and do not address the rejected applicants. Thus, the literature review reveals a lack of insights regarding online product testing programs, and especially concerning rejected applicants.

Although rejections are widespread in everyday life and everyone has encountered them multiple times, defining a rejection is challenging. Its definition depends on the context in which it occurs. In social psychology, rejections appear as ostracism or social exclusion, manifesting as rejection in interpersonal relationships. Due to their long-standing presence, these forms of rejection have already been promptly examined with respect to their effects and influencing factors. In human resource management, rejections occur in the form of declined job applications, whose effects and influencing factors have also been thoroughly analyzed. In marketing, however, rejections appear in three different forms—stockouts, rejection of consumer ideas, and loss in a competition or game. The most common phenomenon, stockouts, provides the most insights into the effects of rejection and the factors influencing its perception. The other two forms of rejection, by contrast, have only been considered to a limited extent. Rejections in online product testing programs, however, have not yet been studied. Thus, there is also a lack of research findings in this area. Furthermore, studies on rejections in the various contexts recognize both negative and positive effects. These effects are often dependent on influencing factors. Due to the lack of studies on rejections in online product testing programs, it is therefore also unclear whether rejections have a negative or positive impact on rejected applicants and which factors exert an influence.

Accordingly, this study aims to address the research gap regarding rejections in online product testing programs. There is a lack of theoretical considerations and empirical investigations examining the effects of rejections in online product testing programs. The present study seeks to highlight the need for research into the relevant psychological mechanisms that influence the effects of a rejection. Ultimately, it is of central importance for both marketing research and marketing practice to understand how rejection changes the behavior of rejected applicants and under what conditions the effect of a rejection occurs.

Development of the Research Model 3

This chapter derives the research model. To this end, an exploratory interview study is conducted at the outset. The aim is to gain initial insights into the potential effects of rejections in online product testing programs and to support the development of hypotheses. In addition, attribution theory and the commitment-consistency principle are used as theoretical foundations. First, the exploratory interview study is presented (**Sect. 3.1**). This is followed by an explanation of the theoretical foundations (**Sect. 3.2**), before the hypotheses are derived (**Sect. 3.3**).

3.1 Exploratory Qualitative Survey

To gain initial insights into the consequences of a rejection in a product testing program for purchase intention and the intention to spread negative word-of-mouth, an exploratory interview study is conducted. Following Eggert, Steinhoff, and Witte (2019), this study, together with attribution theory and the commitment-consistency principle, is subsequently used to develop the research model. The study objective is first outlined (**Sect. 3.1.1**), followed by a rationale for the chosen research design (**Sect. 3.1.2**). The implementation (**Sect. 3.1.3**) and the selection and composition of the sample (**Sect. 3.1.4**) are then described. The analysis of results is presented last (**Sect. 3.1.5**).

K. L. Küpper, *Negative and Positive Effects of Rejections in Online Product Testing Programs*, https://doi.org/10.1007/978-3-658-49277-9_3

3.1.1 Study Objective

The exploratory interview study pursues three main objectives: First, it seeks to examine whether a rejection in a product testing program can influence the future behavior of rejected applicants and thus alter the relationship between the company and the applicant. Furthermore, it aims to determine how the thoughts and feelings of rejected applicants change and whether this is reflected in changes in attitudes and behavior. In this way, both potential negative and positive consequences for companies that issue rejections as part of product testing programs can be identified. By conducting open-ended interviews with a large number of applicants for various product testing programs and exploring their experiences, a broad insight into a wide range of test programs is also obtained. This empirical approach is appropriate, as it allows for the investigation of presumed causal relationships and influencing factors (Gläser/Laudel 2010, p. 24 ff.). By combining the findings from the exploratory study with theoretical insights, the research model and hypotheses can subsequently be developed in a targeted manner.

3.1.2 Rationale for the Research Design

To gain initial insights in a largely unexplored research field, an **exploratory qualitative interview study** can be conducted (Mayring 2023, p. 60). Exploration refers to "the investigation of an unfamiliar area of life within a flexible and reflective approach, whereby results concerning individual data and their interrelations, as well as the methodological steps for their collection and verification, are continuously reflected upon and may be adjusted during the research process" (Lamnek/Krell 2016, p. 49 f.). An exploratory study is therefore particularly suitable at the beginning of a research project to gain an initial understanding of the issue based on real data (Lamnek/Krell 2016, p. 49 f.). The aim of an exploratory study is to foster hypothesis and theory development and, following the study, to be able to narrow down the research subject (Döring/Bortz 2016, p. 612). In this research method, it is especially important that the researcher acts without bias and with openness, being willing to review and, if necessary, revise their own conceptions. Exploration is characterized by the fact that it is not tied to any specific technique and includes any ethically acceptable approach (Lamnek/Krell 2016, p. 49 f.).

Qualitative data collection is often chosen for exploration, followed by a quantitative study. This approach is known as the mixed-methods approach and is also applied in this study (Kuckartz 2014, p. 81). A mixed-methods approach allows the advantages of both quantitative and qualitative studies to be combined, thereby providing new impetus for empirical research (Foscht/Angerer/Swoboda 2007, p. 258). One commonly used method of qualitative analysis is the interview. This method offers several advantages over other qualitative research methods, such as observation. On the one hand, the interpretation of texts in research is already well advanced; on the other hand, information from interviews is authentically unfiltered, intersubjectively comprehensible, and reproducible (Lamnek/Krell 2016, p. 313).

In empirical research, the term *qualitative interviews* refers to a group of procedures that can vary in different directions (Mey/Mruck 2011, p. 259). The choice of procedure can, for example, be based on the degree of structuring and standardization of the interview process. In highly structured interviews, both the interviewer and the interviewee are given little freedom, and the interview follows a predetermined structure, often with predefined answer options. In less structured interviews, the interviewer and interviewee have more freedom in conducting the interview (Klandt/Heidenreich 2017, p. 135; Mayring 2023, p. 60; Mey/Mruck 2011, p. 259 f.). Another aspect in selecting the procedure is the format of the interview. Here, a distinction can be made between oral interviews, such as personal interviews, and written interviews, for example by sending out questionnaires. In recent years, conducting surveys via the Internet has become increasingly popular (Klandt/Heidenreich 2017, p. 135).

3.1.3 Implementation

A standardized questionnaire was developed for the interviews and distributed to participants in written form via the internet. As a result, the degree of structuring and standardization in this study is high. Each participant was asked the same open-ended questions. One advantage of standardized interviews is the high comparability of responses. The potential for errors due to the questions is minimized, as every participant receives the same questions in the same order (Mey/Mruck 2011, p. 259 f.; Lamnek/Krell 2016, p. 323). The study was conducted as individual interviews, meaning that each participant received the questions alone and was expected to answer independently. This structure is standard practice in qualitative research (Lamnek/Krell 2016, p. 324). The questions were formulated in an open-ended style. Participants were free in how they expressed their answers and did not have to fit into any predetermined response scheme (Mayring 2023, p. 60; Lamnek/Krell 2016, p. 326). This ensures that rejected applicants can freely express all their thoughts and feelings, and that no potential effects of rejections in product testing programs remain undiscovered.

The interview study was conducted as a written survey, which was distributed to participants via the online platform Prolific. Prolific is a commercial crowdworking platform used for conducting online research. The platform is used to recruit participants for social and economic scientific experiments (Palan/Schitter 2018, p. 22 f.). The reason for conducting the survey online was the need to recruit rejected product testers. Since applications for product testing programs are submitted online, the choice of the internet as a contact medium was appropriate (Klandt/Heidenreich 2017, p. 151 f.). Because the survey was distributed via a link, the survey was asynchronous. This has the advantage that participants can answer the questions at their own convenience, making it easy to include participants from other countries. At the same time, participants do not feel pressured to respond immediately, but can take their time to formulate their answers. This is especially beneficial for nervous or easily influenced participants. Distributing the survey link via an online platform also ensures that participants remain completely anonymous. This enables open responses to questions, even on sensitive topics (Gnambs/Batinic 2011, p. 388 ff.; Klandt/Heidenreich 2017, p. 151 f.). With online interviews, the responses are immediately available in digital form after the survey and do not require transcription (Döring/Bortz 2016, p. 375).

For the implementation, a total of two surveys were programmed using the SoSci Survey website and then posted on Prolific. The first survey served solely to select suitable participants. Since it was not possible to pre-select registered Prolific members based on their experience with product testing programs, an initial survey was conducted. In this survey, 600 participants were asked whether they had ever applied for a product test and subsequently received a rejection from the company. If so, they were asked to briefly name the product testing program and the company. They were informed in advance that this survey consisted of only these two questions and was solely intended to identify suitable candidates for the subsequent in-depth survey. Based on their previous experience, 112 participants qualified for the subsequent interview study.

These 112 participants were then invited to take part in the survey, of whom 102 completed the interview study. At the beginning, participants were informed that the study concerned their experiences with product testing programs and were asked to write as openly and in as much detail as possible about both their positive and negative thoughts and feelings. They were assured that there were no wrong answers and that all data would be kept anonymous and used solely for scientific purposes. When answering the questions, participants were asked to recall the most recent rejection they had received from a product testing program.

They were then asked about their thoughts and feelings following the rejection, for example with the questions: "Did the rejection create negative feelings about the company or the product test? Please describe these negative feelings and explain why you feel this way," "Did you experience feelings of skepticism after the rejection? Please describe your feelings and explain why you feel this way," and "Did you experience feelings of desire to own the product? Please describe your feelings and explain why you feel this way."

When designing the questionnaire, care was taken to ensure that participants could express their thoughts and feelings. To this end, open-ended questions were asked that were simple and direct in their wording. Participants were encouraged to describe their experiences and to provide as much detail as possible. Leading questions that might suggest a particular answer were completely avoided. Factual and closed questions were used only sparingly (Döring/Bortz 2016, p. 403), for example at the end of the questionnaire, where participants were asked how often they had already received rejections. Finally, they provided some sociodemographic information. On average, it took about 15 minutes to answer all the questions.

3.1.4 Sample Selection and Composition

To gain initial insights into the effects of rejections in product testing programs, a sample was required that included only individuals who had previously applied for a product test and subsequently received a rejection. Since no pre-screening filter on Prolific allowed for this selection, a brief preliminary survey was conducted. In addition, available pre-screening filters were used to recruit participants from the United Kingdom who regularly shop online. The 600 participants who took part in the first survey received a compensation of £0.13. The 102 participants who had already experienced rejections in product testing programs and reported on their experiences in the subsequent survey received £1.88. Among the 102 participants, the youngest was 22 years old and the oldest was 79 years old. The mean age of the sample was 43.29 years. 75% of the participants were female, 21.9% were male, and 3.1% did not disclose their gender.

3.1.5 Analysis of Results

The analysis of results consists of two subsections. First, the evaluation method is presented (**Sect. 3.1.5.1**), followed by the presentation of the results (**Sect. 3.1.5.2**).

3.1.5.1 Evaluation Method

The evaluation of the qualitative interviews is based on the *Grounded Theory* by Strauss (1998, p. 50 ff.) and the *content analysis* according to Kuckartz (2016, p. 164 f.). Figure 3.1 illustrates the analysis process of the qualitative interviews.

The foundation of Grounded Theory is the systematic analysis of empirical data. Strauss refers to his approach as Grounded Theory "because its focus is on generating a theory and on the data in which this theory is grounded" (Strauss, 1998, p. 50). In the **first coding step**, an interview is analyzed openly, usually sentence by sentence, to systematically organize the statements. Within the framework of Grounded Theory, categories are formed. These categories are derived from various indicators identified by the researcher in the interviews, which are then compared and combined. If certain indicators are similar in terms of events or behavioral patterns, they can be grouped into a coded category. In addition to categories, the researcher can also form subcategories that further subdivide the main category. During open coding, indicators and categories are initially recorded provisionally. In the **second coding step**, coding is carried out based on Strauss's framework. He suggests focusing in particular on conditions, interactions between actors, strategies and tactics, and consequences (Strauss 1998, p. 57).

In marketing research, it is also common to analyze interviews with regard to relational mediators and outcome variables (Palmatier et al. 2006, p. 137). Accordingly, this study primarily codes for psychological mechanisms triggered by a rejection in a product testing program, changes in attitude of the rejected applicant, and the consequences of the rejection in terms of the rejected applicant's behavior. By combining Grounded Theory with the content analysis method of Kuckartz (2016, p. 164 f.), it is possible in the **third coding step** to form main and subcategories both deductively and inductively. This allows previously established findings on the effects of rejections to be incorporated into the category formation. However, the researcher remains open to other inductively derived categories that emerge from the material. The interviews are analyzed and coded until no further categories can be identified and saturation is reached. The results are then presented by reproducing expert statements using relevant

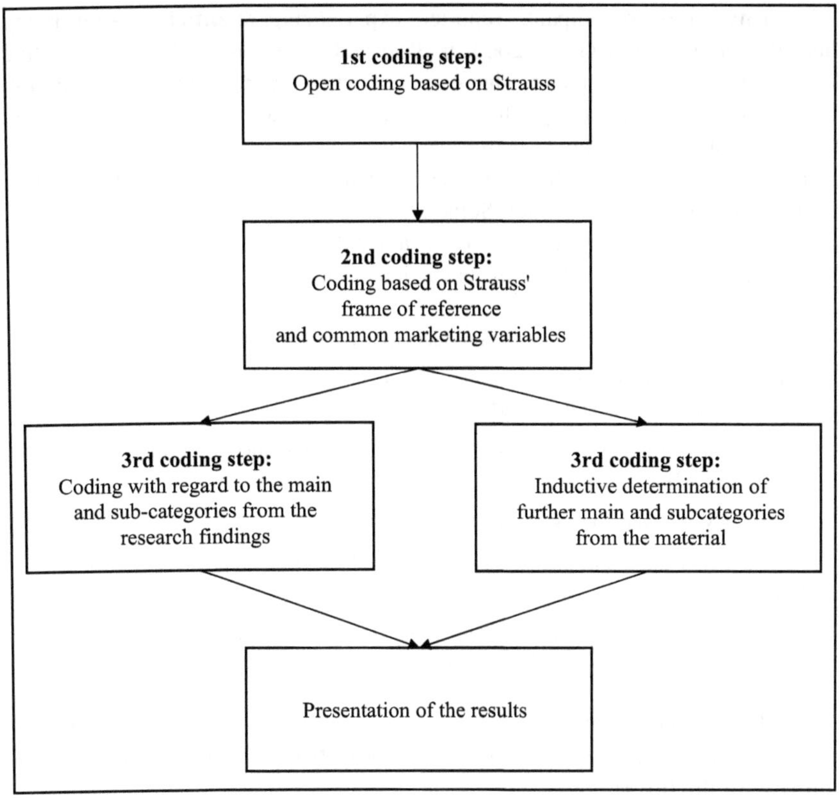

Fig. 3.1 Analysis process of the exploratory qualitative study. (*Source:* Own illustration)

quotations. This type of presentation is chosen to enable the reader to follow the reasoning and draw their own conclusions (Gläser/Laudel 2010, p. 273 f.).

3.1.5.2 Results

The qualitative interviews provided initial insights into the psychological mechanisms, the behavior of rejected applicants, and other influencing factors that occur following a rejection in a product testing program.

In many cases, participants reported experiencing **skepticism** after being rejected. Forehand and Grier (2003, p. 350) and Steinhoff (2014, p. 96) define skepticism as a negative feeling that can arise when a person experiences doubt, uncertainty, and mistrust regarding the sincerity of another person or entity. Rejected applicants question whether the company actually sends out the advertised test products or whether it is merely a marketing campaign designed to generate attention for the product. Some also suspect that the real aim of the campaign is simply to collect customer data rather than to conduct genuine product testing, and thus the product test is not carried out properly.

> "I do wonder if they really have the products to test they said they do." (*female, 42*)
>
> "I never get chosen and always fill out so many questions for nothing. Do they even give out test products?" (*female, 40*)
>
> "I was not sure if the product test was real or whether they just wanted my information." (*male, 42*)
>
> "I think they just wanted to grab my data." (*female, 38*)
>
> "I was directed straight to their website which made me feel skeptical about if it was just an advertising ploy." (*female, 59*)
>
> "I felt shortchanged by them, I spent time answering my questions only to be rejected at the end. I don't think I was even really properly considered." (*female, 42*)

This feeling of skepticism often leads rejected applicants to develop a **negative attitude** toward the company and to **avoid any further interaction with the company in the future**.

> "I would not try to apply again." (*female, 55*)
>
> "I would likely consider avoiding their products in future." (*male, 32*)

However, the interviews also revealed positive consequences of rejections in product testing programs. For some participants, the application and subsequent rejection led to a sense of **commitment** to the company. Participants appreciated the product test and the company's interest in consumer opinions. Through the application process, they felt connected to the company and one step closer to the product.

> "I felt more positive towards these companies as they want to hear what people think of their products and listen to consumers to make their products better." (*female, 52*)

> "The company had nothing personal against me. I appreciate that they do product testing and learn about new products through that, even if I don't get accepted. That way I can decide for myself afterwards whether to buy it or not." (*female, 38*)

> " [The rejection] prompted me to investigate buying and actively search out the products on online shopping and in store. I wanted to try them and it reminded me and to check if any new brands, box sizes or price being more favorable since last checking maybe a YEAR ago!" (*male, 32*)

This sense of commitment had a positive effect on the rejected applicants' attitude toward the company. After the rejection, they remained positively disposed toward the company and continued to be loyal customers. This positive attitude subsequently led to a higher purchase intention among rejected applicants. Many participants reported that they **purchased the product** because they still wanted to try it, even after being rejected.

> "I was intrigued to try the test product." (*female, 24*)

> "I didn't know about the product prior to the test so was excited to find out about it and would probably still purchase when its available to buy." (*female, 33*)

> "I still enjoy the brand and would like to own the product." (*female, 28*)

> "Through the application, I got involved with the product and the company. After the rejection, I looked for other test products of the company." (*female, 42*)

> "I still believe that this is a good company." (*male, 41*)

> "I remained loyal to the company and bought it myself." (*male, 42*)

In addition to the psychological mechanisms and their effects on the attitudes and behavior of rejected applicants, two relevant contextual factors also emerged from the analysis. The first influencing factor is the **price of the test product**. It affects both perceived skepticism and perceived commitment. Applicants find it logical that the company incurs higher implementation costs for product tests involving higher-priced products. These higher costs need to be compensated, and participants suspect that they would react **even more skeptically**.

> "[In case of an expensive test product, I would] probably [be] more skeptical because there would have been more investment on their [i.e. the manufacturers'] part." (*female, 31*)

This skepticism could even lead to participants not applying at all.

"I don't think I would apply for a more expensive product as more people would be applying for this and the chances of getting it would be even slimmer than a cheaper product. I think that the companies then rather offer even fewer test products, if there are any at all." (*female, 57*)

On the other hand, higher-priced test products lead to a **stronger commitment**, and it is assumed that companies then select their testers even more carefully.

"I have a higher desire to own the product" (*male, 30*)

"I know there are limited availability of products and they choose most suitable and even more carefully if the price is high" (*female, 38*)

"More expensive products are seen to be exclusive, so there may be a feeling of missing out." (*female, 56*)

"It would make me feel much more positively towards the company." (*female, 37*)

This higher commitment leads to higher purchase intentions among rejected applicants:

"Still buy the [more expensive] product if I wanted it." (*female, 45*)

The second contextual factor influencing the consequences of rejections is the **number of previous rejections**. The interviews again show an effect of the number of rejections on both skepticism and commitment. It becomes clear that participants apply for product tests more frequently and are therefore rejected more often. With repeated rejections, rejected applicants increasingly question the credibility and proper execution of the product test.

"I get a little more annoyed with them each time I get rejected." (*female, 52*)

"I […] feel more despondent and have little trust in the company." (*female, 50*)

"Feel I was wasting time and wonder if the company were genuine." (*female, 53*)

This **higher level of skepticism** leads to a greater likelihood that rejected applicants will avoid the company and no longer apply for product tests:

"I would probably feel like not bothering to apply in future." (*female, 24*)

"I would just stop using them completely." (*female, 43*)

At the same time, some applicants show **increasing commitment** to the company as the number of applications rises:

> "Rejections would not deter me." (*female, 56*)
>
> "It's desirable to be a tester." (*male, 42)*
>
> "Every rejection increases my desire be taken next time." (*male, 22*)

This higher commitment leads to further applications, even if applicants are rejected multiple times:

> "I would still continue to make applications. Rejections would not deter me." (*female, 56*)
>
> "I will try again if they need reviewers for other products." (*female, 59*)
>
> "I would still continue to make applications." (*female, 56*)
>
> "I ended up applying for more out of a desire to be more successful going forward." (*male, 30*)

The exploratory interview study was able to confirm the initial assumption that a rejection in a product testing program can potentially influence the feelings and behavior of rejected applicants. A rejection can affect the perceived skepticism and commitment of rejected applicants. These psychological mechanisms can in turn influence the attitude of rejected applicants toward the company and impact their behavior. Nevertheless, the exploratory interview study provides only initial indications that need to be examined in more detail in further studies. For this reason, the findings of the study are used below to be further developed and substantiated with theoretical foundations. The resulting research model will then be tested in further empirical studies, and the consequences of rejections in product testing programs will be explored in greater depth.

3.2 Theoretical Foundations

The following chapter presents the theoretical foundations. First, attribution theory (**Sect. 3.2.1**) is explained in detail, followed by an explanation of the commitment-consistency principle (**Sect. 3.2.2**).

3.2.1 Attribution Theory

People try to understand their own behavior and that of others by attributing possible reasons. According to attribution theory, people arrive at causal explanations by inferring the cause of an event. The theory posits that the starting point of all human action is the question of reasons, i.e., the question of "why?" (Garms-Homolová 2021, p. 34). The development of the theory goes back to Heider (1958) and is now considered an umbrella term for a range of contributions in social psychology (Jones/Davis 1965; Weiner 1985; Weiner 1986). The following explanations of the theory are based on the works of Heider (1985) and Weiner (1985; 1986), as these approaches also consider the effects on human experience and behavior.

Attribution means "finding explanations for one's own and others' behavior, attributing characteristics or states to oneself and others" (Oliver 2010, p. 295; Parkinson 2007, p. 71). In attribution theory, there is an observer who observes a situation and what happens, and an actor. In some situations, the observer can also be the actor. In this case, it is called self-attribution. Attribution research deals with the conclusions drawn by the observer when observing the actor. In this process, the observer makes an attribution by trying to establish a causal relationship to explain the actor's behavior. Thus, people try to understand and explain both the behavior of others and their own behavior (Heider 1958, p. 5; Parkinson 2007, p. 76). Establishing causality and the resulting conclusions offer two advantages for people: Through attribution, people gain a sense of understanding. This sense of understanding alleviates fear and provides a feeling of security in dealing with their current situation and environment. Second, by uncovering reasons, people gain a certain degree of control over future events and can better predict future behavior (Weiner 1985, p. 548; Parkinson 2007, p. 76).

Attribution depends on the presumed causes of the event. Heider (1985) makes an important distinction between "**internal**" and "**external**" causes. This determines whether the cause of a particular action lies within the person performing it (e.g., based on intention, ability, or effort) or is due to external factors (such as timing or circumstances, the involvement of other people, or chance). In internal attribution, the cause always lies within the person, whereas in external or situational attribution, the cause lies in the situation (Heider 1985, p. 82; Stroebe/Jonas/Hewstone 2003, p. 217).

The theory was later expanded by Heider (1985) to include two additional factors: stability and controllability. These factors were incorporated and further developed by Weiner in the development of the multidimensional approach.

Weiner (1985; 1986) refers to the distinction between internal and external attribution as **locus** and uses this as the first causal dimension in his three-dimensional model. The other two causal dimensions, which are also dichotomous and examined in more detail by him, are **stability** and **controllability**. Stability, as the second causal dimension, describes whether the causes of an event are relatively constant, predictable, and enduring, or variable, unpredictable, and unique. The third causal dimension, controllability, concerns whether the factor is controllable by the actor or not.

Table 3.1 presents the model by Weiner (1979; 1985; 1986) and illustrates the academic context referenced in this explanation and by Weiner.

If the causal dimensions of locus, stability, and controllability are considered using the example of a student taking an exam, a good grade can be attributed either to the person themselves (internal cause) or to the situation (external cause). Passing an exam can, in terms of the stability dimension, be traced back to stable internal reasons (e.g., ability or aptitude) or unstable internal reasons (e.g., particularly high study effort). For external causes, stable external reasons (e.g., persistent situational factors or the ease of the tasks) or unstable external reasons (e.g., temporary situational factors or luck) can also be attributed. In the dimension of controllability, the causes for passing an exam may be consciously controllable or uncontrollable by the student. If a student invests a great deal of effort in studying, the internally attributed reason can be perceived as controllable. However, if success in the exam is attributed to the student's aptitude, this may be perceived as uncontrollable by the student. For external causes, there may also be controllable reasons for passing an exam (e.g., help from a fellow student) or uncontrollable reasons (e.g., luck) (Parkinson 2007, p. 85).

Table 3.1 Causal model according to Weiner (1979; 1985; 1986)

	Internal Cause		External Cause	
	Stable	Unstable	Stable	Unstable
Controllable	Ability (e.g., knowledge, skill)	Effort	Permanent situational and social resources (e.g., social contacts, financial assets)	Temporarily available situational and social resources (e.g., advice, support)
Uncontrollable	Aptitude (e.g., intelligence)	Energy	Ease or difficulty of the task	Luck/chance

Source: Adapted from Steinhoff, 2014, p. 86 and Parkinson, 2007, p. 85.

The entire attribution process that an observer undergoes can be illustrated in a model (Weiner 1985, p. 565). The model comprises five sequential steps: the event and its evaluation as the starting point, event-dependent emotions, the attribution process, attribution-dependent emotions, and behavioral consequences. The model is shown in Fig. 3.2.

The model of the attribution process begins with an event and its evaluation as the **starting point**. The observer can assess the event as a success or failure. The resulting **basic event-dependent emotions** (step 2) can be positive in the

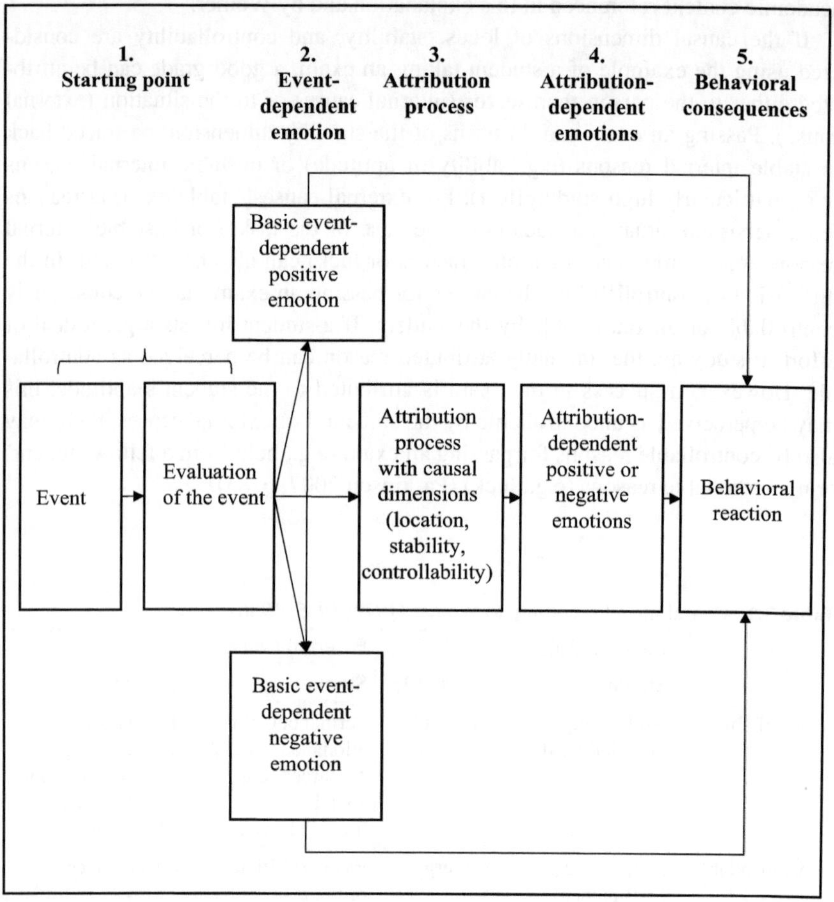

Fig. 3.2 Attribution process. (*Source:* Adapted from Weiner, 1985, p. 565; 1986, p. 162)

case of success or negative in the case of failure. In the case of success, the emotion is often joy, while in the case of failure it is frustration or sadness. However, if the result of the evaluation is unexpected, negative, or particularly personally relevant, the **attribution process** (step 3) is also initiated. The attribution of the event follows the three causal dimensions already described: locus, stability, and controllability. As a result of the attribution process, **attribution-dependent emotions** (step 4) occur. These are largely determined by the preceding attribution process and the causal dimensions. The locus dimension, for example, can elicit emotions such as pride, whereas the stability dimension can cause emotions such as hope or hopelessness. If an observer feels exposed to an uncontrollable event, this can lead to emotions such as anger or shame. In the fifth step, the event-dependent and attribution-dependent emotions together lead to **behavioral consequences** for the observer. The behavior derived from the resulting emotions can influence both the individual's own actions and the behavior of others. Since event-dependent and attribution-dependent emotions do not always have to coincide, behavior is often a mixture of both types of emotions (Weiner 1985, p. 560 f.).

However, the attribution process can also fail. There are three possible reasons for this: First, negative information can lead to a disproportionate judgment bias (Feinberg/Meoli-Stanton/Gable 1996, p. 64). Second, incorrect attribution can occur if the observer is not aware of all relevant influencing factors of the events and draws causal conclusions solely based on experience (Parkinson 2007, p. 80 f.). Third, incorrect attributions or self-serving attributional biases may also occur. These are defined as follows: "Motivated distortions of attributional inferences that serve to maintain or enhance self-esteem" (Parkinson 2007, p. 101). Consequently, this involves motivated distortion by the observer. Events and causal conclusions can thus be attributed in a way that is personally more favorable to the observer. In the academic context, this results in attributing a good grade to innate abilities (self-enhancing bias). In the case of failure, the attribution may be distorted so that the failure is attributed solely to an unfair exam question (self-protective bias). In general, this means that the observer tends to protect themselves and their self-image by not carrying out the attribution process correctly (Parkinson 2007, p. 101 f.).

3.2.2 Commitment-Consistency Principle

People strive throughout their lives to behave consistently (Cialdini 2007; Festinger 1957). Cialdini (2007, pp. 43 ff.) explains this feeling in a chapter of his book entitled "Commitment and Consistency." Based on this chapter, the commitment-consistency principle refers to situations in which a person remains loyal to a decision, even when it is no longer rational to continue on that path. Once a person has made a decision, they feel pressured to act in accordance with that decision in the future. Even if the person appeared cautious and uncertain before making the decision, it is likely that after making a firm choice, they will appear confident and optimistic. Rationally, it is not possible to determine in such a short time whether the person has made the right or wrong decision, yet they feel more secure and optimistic that everything will turn out well. According to Cialdini (2007, p. 43), there is a desire to be (and appear) consistent with what one has already done. After making a decision, the person comes under personal and interpersonal pressure, which can lead to irrational future decisions (Cialdini 2007, p. 43).

To illustrate this pressure, Cialdini (2007, p. 43) provides an example from his neighborhood: His neighbor had a partner with whom she lived. According to Cialdini, the relationship was always complicated. After many conflicts, the neighbor ended the relationship and her partner moved out. After some time, her ex-partner contacted her again and wanted to resume the relationship. He promised her that he would improve his behavior towards her. Cialdini's neighbor took her ex-partner back, and it became clear that the situation they lived in from that point on was no different from before the breakup. However, the neighbor felt more emotionally connected to her partner than ever before. She reported that, because she had consciously chosen the relationship, she realized whom she truly loved. Cialdini's neighbor was more committed to the relationship than ever. Although the conditions under which she made her choice were never fulfilled, she was happier because she had actively decided to take this step. According to Cialdini (2007), it is common for people to deceive themselves in order to be happy with the decisions they have made (Cialdini 2007, pp. 43 f.).

Festinger (1957) had already identified the desire for consistency as a central motivator of human behavior. This desire can trigger a kind of automatism. This automatism is also referred to as "blind consistency" and can lead to both **positive and negative consequences** for the individual, as shown in Table 3.2.

Among the **positive consequences** of consistent behavior is that individuals who act consistently are valued in society. A high degree of consistency is often associated with personal and intellectual strength, whereas people whose opinions do not align with their actions are less respected, and breaking one's word is considered a negative personal trait. Such individuals are seen as indecisive, confused, duplicitous, or even mentally unstable. In addition, consistent behavior also benefits both the individual and society. Consistent behavior provides

Table 3.2 Possible consequences of consistent behavior

Positive consequences	Negative consequences
Is valued by society.	The person may act against their own interests and well-being.
Provides clear orientation for the individual and society.	The person may be exploited by other parties.
No further reflection required, resulting in less time spent on future decisions.	The person is more easily manipulated.
Enables quick responses to everyday situations.	
Avoidance of unwelcome thoughts and facts.	

Source: Own illustration.

society with clear orientation (Cialdini 2007, pp. 44 f.). For the individual, consistent behavior means that once a decision has been made, there is no need to reconsider further decisions or situations. There is no need to review additional facts or weigh further pros and cons. The person continues to act in line with their previous decision, saving considerable time otherwise spent on reflection and evaluation. This behavior is therefore an efficient method, as it allows the individual to respond quickly and easily to complex everyday problems without expending mental resources. Consistency appears attractive to society because a person does not have to confront unwelcome thoughts or facts if they do not reflect on the decision or situation at all. In this way, individuals protect themselves from thoughts and realizations that could potentially be negative for them (Cialdini 2007, p. 46). However, consistent behavior can also have **negative consequences**. Due to the high regard for consistency in society and the aforementioned benefits for the individual, the desire for consistency can become so strong that it leads people to do things that are contrary to their own interests or even endanger them. In an experiment by Moriarty (1975, pp. 370 ff.), it was shown that people only stopped a would-be thief after being asked to watch over valuables (Moriarty 1975, pp. 370 ff.). Furthermore, this behavior can lead to others exploiting the individual and taking advantage of the fact that decisions are not carefully considered. For those who simply want to impose their will, it is easy to manipulate a person who behaves blindly consistently. Companies, among others, attempt to exploit this in order to increase sales (Cialdini 2007, pp. 49 ff.).

To understand the urge for consistent behavior, it is necessary to know what ultimately triggers such behavior. Social psychologists see commitment as the cause of the mechanism behind consistent behavior (Cialdini 2007; Freedman/Fraser 1966). Once a person has been persuaded to commit to something, consistent behavior can be triggered. This commitment can be seen as a kind of attitude that is further developed through consistent behavior (Baca-Motes et al. 2013, p. 1071; Cialdini 2007, p. 189). Such a connection between consistency and commitment is now widely recognized, and companies and political parties also use tactics to elicit commitment, for example, to obtain donations or win voters (Cialdini 2007, pp. 55 f.; Howard 1990, pp. 1185 ff.; Sherman 1980, pp. 211 ff.).

3.3 Derivation of the Hypotheses

The following section deduces hypotheses regarding the effects of rejections in online product testing programs on the psychological processes and behavior of rejected applicants, based on the results of the exploratory qualitative study and the theoretical approaches presented. In the first step, the negative effects of a rejection are derived (**Sect. 3.3.1**). Subsequently, hypotheses on the positive effects of a rejection are formulated (**Sect. 3.2.2**). The moderating effect of the test product's price is then incorporated into the hypotheses (**Sect. 3.3.3**), and finally, the effect of the frequency of rejection is hypothesized (**Sect. 3.3.4**). In the last step, an overview of the hypotheses is provided and the research model is summarized (**Sect. 3.3.5**).

3.3.1 Negative Effects of a Rejection

The negative effects of a rejection within the context of product testing programs can be explained using attribution theory. According to attribution theory (Kelley 1973), people make causal explanations by inferring the causes of events. Studies have shown that initiating an attribution process is a cognitive tactic to recover from rejection (Wesselmann/Williams 2017, p. 696). However, people can also fail in their assessment of attribution processes (Weiner 1985), and negative information such as a rejection can impair a person's judgment (Feinberg/Meoli-Stanton/Gable, 1996, p. 64).

In terms of attribution theory, there is an actor and an observer. When the applicant receives a rejection from the company, the actor is the company issuing the rejection, and the observer is the applicant for the product test whose application was declined.

The focus, therefore, is on the conclusions drawn by the rejected applicant after receiving the company's rejection. Following the rejection, the applicant engages in attribution by attempting to establish a causal link to explain the company's behavior. This is done to better cope with the situation and to regain a sense of control over the uncertain circumstances.

The attribution process, as outlined by Weiner (1985), is illustrated in Fig. 3.3.

The process begins with the company's rejection as the starting point. This event is evaluated by the rejected applicant. In order to draw conclusions about the reasons for the rejection, the attribution process starts with an analysis of the situation based on the causal dimensions of locus, stability, and controllability. First, it is assessed whether the cause is internal or external. Since people tend to protect themselves and find it easier to attribute negative events to external causes (Parkinson 2007, p. 101), the rejected applicant is also likely to assume external reasons for the rejection and attribute them to the company. This can be seen as a form of self-serving attributional bias. Consequently, the rejected applicant reframes the perceived situation in a way that preserves their self-esteem. For this reason, the applicant does not attribute the rejection to themselves or their own behavior, but rather to the company that issued the rejection, regardless of whether this attribution is accurate or not.

When assessing the stability of the situation, the rejected applicant concludes that the event is unstable, variable, and unpredictable, as it could just as easily have had a positive outcome and the decision was based on rules that are not transparent to the applicant. The decision was entirely dependent on the company and therefore cannot be considered constant or permanent. The rejected applicant thus perceives the rejection not as a regular, recurring measure, but rather as a

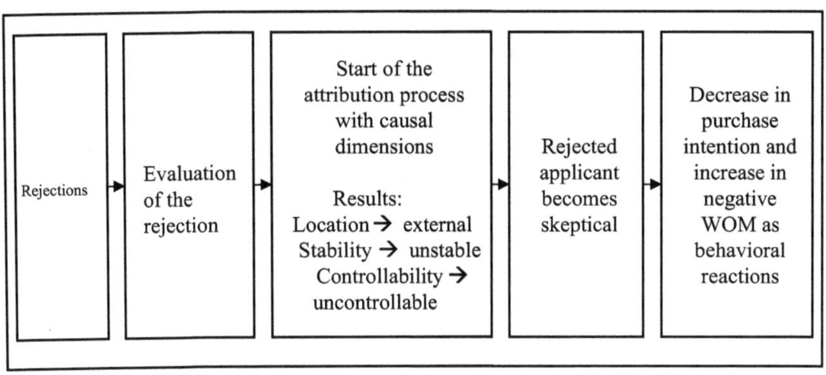

Fig. 3.3 Attribution process following a rejection. *(Source:* Own illustration)

random, possibly one-off action by the company. The company's approach is therefore seen as unstable, variable, and unpredictable.

In evaluating controllability, it can be assumed that the applicant has little to no control over the outcome of their application. If the application requires information about the person or their motivation, the applicant can at most try to respond in a way that appeals to the company and presents them as a good product tester. However, since the applicant does not know the selection criteria, it is nearly impossible to tailor responses accordingly. The actual selection of testers is made solely by the company and therefore cannot be influenced by the applicant. As a result, the event is evaluated as **external, unstable, and uncontrollable**.

The resulting emotions are therefore negative. The self-serving attributional bias and the perceived instability lead the applicant to question the company's motives. The rejected applicant tries to understand the company's true intentions behind the product test. It is possible that they suspect hidden interests as the reason for the rejection. Companies are profit-oriented, and product tests are considered an expensive marketing tool, as the company provides the test products free of charge (Jain/Mahajan/Muller 1995, p. 125; Yao et al. 2017, p. 599). Therefore, after a rejection, an applicant may be skeptical as to whether the company truly intended to provide the promised test products, or whether the product test was merely used for advertising purposes or to collect applicant data. Interviews with rejected applicants have already revealed skepticism as a consequence of rejection. Some respondents doubted whether test products even existed and suspected that the product test was used solely for advertising or for collecting consumer data:

> "I was directed straight to their website which made me feel skeptical about if it was just an advertising ploy." *(female, 59).*

According to the theory, the final step in the attribution process is the impact of emotions on behavior. It is likely that, as a result of their skepticism, rejected applicants will respond negatively toward the company (Eggert/Steinhoff/Garnefeld 2015, p. 210 ff.; Koslow 2000, p. 250). They are more likely to avoid the company and not purchase the test product, and instead speak negatively about the company within their circle of friends and family. The structured qualitative interviews confirm such negative attitudes and behavioral intentions toward the company:

> "I would not try to apply again." *(female, 55).*

Based on attribution theory and the results of the qualitative interviews, the following hypotheses are proposed: that rejections in product tests increase skepticism, which in turn leads to a decrease in applicants' purchase intentions and an increase in the intention to spread negative word-of-mouth:

H1a: The rejection of applications in a product testing program reduces the purchase intentions of rejected applicants (compared to non-applicants), mediated by an increase in perceived skepticism.

H1b: The rejection of applications in a product testing program increases the intention to spread negative word-of-mouth among rejected applicants (compared to non-applicants), mediated by an increase in perceived skepticism.

3.3.2 Positive Effects of a Rejection

The positive effects of a rejection within the context of product testing programs can be explained using the commitment-consistency principle. According to this principle (Cialdini 2007), people strive to behave consistently. Consistent behavior is often advantageous for individuals and is valued by society. However, it can also have negative consequences and lead to irrational behavior (Cialdini 2007, pp. 44 ff.; Moriarty 1975, pp. 370 ff.).

When a consumer is interested in a product and a product test and applies to participate, this is due to their commitment. The individual actively decides to apply. By submitting the application, they enter into an active commitment, which can trigger the mechanism of consistent behavior. Making commitments increases applicants' confidence in their attitudes (Dunn/Schweiter 2005, pp. 745 f.; Gopinath/Nyer 2009, pp. 65 f.) and is an effective and lasting predictor of future behavior (Lokhorst et al. 2013, p. 29; Park et al. 2010, pp. 14 f.). As a result of the application, the applicant may now feel a desire to behave consistently with their previous actions. Consistent behavior is valued in society, and a high degree of consistency is often associated with personal and intellectual strength (Cialdini 2007, pp. 44 f.). The applicant wants to be attributed these positive qualities as a result of their consistent behavior. In addition, the commitment to the company also provides the applicant with benefits: since they have made the decision to apply—and especially since initial decisions are usually made with particular care (Urbany/Dickson/Wilkie 1989, p. 208)—they can now "blindly" rely on their decision and do not need to further deliberate about subsequent decisions regarding the company or their interest in the test product.

Based on experiments by Cialdini (2009, pp. 49 ff.), Howard (1990, pp. 1,185 ff.), and Sherman (1980, pp. 211 ff.), which examined the initial creation of commitment in various business contexts, it is even conceivable that companies offering product tests deliberately use these as campaigns to trigger an initial commitment. This initial commitment then sets consistent behavior in motion among applicants. The rejection within the product testing program can further influence the commitment of the rejected applicant. The rejection increases commitment because the unavailability of the test product at that moment makes the product appear even more desirable to the rejected applicant. The unfulfilled desire for the test product leads to further consistent behavior toward the company (Cialdini 2007, p. 189; Hamilton et al. 2019, pp. 533 f.; Suri/Kohli/Monroe 2007, pp. 89 f.). This behavior may manifest as continued interest in the company and further support, for example, in the form of higher purchase intentions or lower intentions to spread negative word-of-mouth (Eggert/Steinhoff/Witte 2019, p. 126; Rehman et al. 2019, pp. 17 f.).

The results of the qualitative survey also showed that rejection after applying increased attitudes and loyalty toward the company due to the perceived commitment. Rejected applicants still want to test and own the product after the rejection because they once actively decided in favor of it:

> "I didn't know about the product prior to the test so was excited to find out about it and would probably still purchase when its available to buy." *(female, 33)* and

> "Through the application, I got involved with the product and the company. After the rejection, I looked for other test products of the company." (*female, 42*).

The qualitative survey also provided further insights into increased commitment following a rejection in the context of an online product testing program. Rejected applicants demonstrate commitment by appreciating companies for conducting product tests and for their interest in consumer opinions and feedback:

> "I appreciate that they do product testing and learn about new products through that, even if I don't get accepted." *(female, 38).*

Based on the social-psychological explanations and findings from the exploratory qualitative survey, the following hypotheses are proposed:

> *H2a: The rejection of applications in a product testing program increases the purchase intentions of rejected applicants (compared to non-applicants), mediated by an increase in perceived commitment.*
> *H2b: The rejection of applications in a product testing program reduces the intention to spread negative word-of-mouth among rejected applicants (compared to non-applicants), mediated by an increase in perceived commitment.*

3.3.3 Moderating Effect of the Test Product's Price

Price can have both a positive and a negative moderating effect on the purchase intention and the intention to spread negative WOM among rejected applicants. According to attribution theory (Kelley 1973), rejected applicants will initiate the attribution process to determine the reasons for the rejection.

They will assume that the costs of a product test are higher for the company when an expensive test product is offered, since the company provides the test product free of charge (Jain/Mahajan/Muller 1995, p. 125; Yao et al. 2017, p. 599). After receiving a rejection, they are more likely to question the product testing program if a high-priced test product was offered, as companies must achieve a high return from the marketing tool to offset the costs of the product test (Adams 1965, p. 281). It is likely that they will suspect hidden motives on the part of the company as the reason for the rejection. They will be **more skeptical** of the company and its marketing activities than in the case of a product test with a less expensive product. As a result of their skepticism, rejected applicants are more likely to avoid the company in the case of a product test with a high-priced test product and subsequently not purchase the test product, but rather tend to speak negatively about the company. This is also reflected in the findings from the exploratory qualitative survey:

> "[In case of an expensive test product, I would] probably [be] more skeptical because there would have been more investment on their [i.e. the manufacturers'] part." *(female, 31)* and
>
> "The companies then [i.e., in case of high-priced test products] rather offer even fewer test products, if there are any at all." *(female, 57).*

At the same time, it is possible that applicants show **higher commitment** after a rejection because a higher-priced product is more desirable for the consumer. They may research the product more thoroughly and consider it longer (Urbany/Dickson/Wilkie 1989, p. 208) before applying for more expensive products. This can lead to an increase in perceived commitment (Ko/Cho/Roberts 2005, p. 61), which is reflected in higher purchase intention and a reduction in the intention to spread negative WOM:

> "More expensive products are seen to be exclusive, so there may be a feeling of missing out." *(female, 56).*

Based on attribution theory, the commitment-consistency principle, and findings from the exploratory qualitative study, the following hypotheses are proposed:

H3a: The negative effect of a rejection in a product testing program among rejected applicants (compared to non-applicants) on purchase intention, mediated by an increase in perceived skepticism, is stronger for high-priced products than for low-priced products.

H3b: The positive effect of a rejection in a product testing program among rejected applicants (compared to non-applicants) on purchase intention, mediated by an increase in perceived commitment, is stronger for high-priced products than for low-priced products.

H3c: The positive effect of a rejection in a product testing program among rejected applicants (compared to non-applicants) on the intention to spread negative word-of-mouth, mediated by an increase in perceived skepticism, is stronger for high-priced products than for low-priced products.

H3d: The negative effect of a rejection in a product testing program among rejected applicants (compared to non-applicants) on the intention to spread negative word-of-mouth, mediated by an increase in perceived commitment, is stronger for high-priced products than for low-priced products.

3.3.4 Effect of the Number of Rejections

The number of rejections can have both a positive and a negative effect on the purchase intention and the intention to spread negative word-of-mouth among rejected applicants. Previous research has shown that repetition, for example in advertising, can have a positive learning effect on individuals. However, this positive effect can turn negative after a certain number of repetitions, with each additional repetition leading to irritation (Kirmani 1997, pp. 84 f.). In the context of job applications, repeated rejections can lead to applicants abandoning further application attempts (Paul/Moser 2001, pp. 83 ff.). Similarly, Fombelle, Bone, and Lemon (2016, pp. 685 f.) found that when submitting additional ideas to a company, the outcome of previous submissions plays an important role. A repeated rejection can cause the rejected applicant to avoid submitting further ideas, as he or she perceives a greater threat to self-esteem (Fombelle/Bone/Lemon 2016, pp. 685 f.). In competitions and sweepstakes as well, the perception of rejection depends on previous experiences (Leclercq/Hammedi/Poncin 2018, p. 93).

In the context of product tests, some applicants may apply multiple times and also be rejected multiple times. This occurs especially in large communities, such as those of dm-drogerie markt or Phillips. In the exploratory qualitative study, the 102 participants had already received an average of 5.9 rejections. Based on attribution theory and the commitment-consistency principle, it can be assumed that the number of rejections influences the effect of rejections on perceived skepticism and perceived commitment.

According to attribution theory, product testers who are repeatedly rejected will increasingly question the product test and become more skeptical. This higher level of skepticism leads to a greater likelihood that rejected applicants will, for example, avoid the company and no longer apply for product tests. This was already evident in the statements of respondents in the exploratory qualitative survey:

> "Feel I was wasting time and wonder if the company were genuine." *(female, 53)*,
>
> "I get a little more annoyed with them each time I get rejected." *(female, 52)*,
>
> "I […] feel more despondent and have little trust in the company." *(female, 50)*, and
>
> "I would probably feel like not bothering to apply in future." *(female, 24)*.

At the same time, based on the commitment-consistency principle, it is possible that applicants who repeatedly apply for a company's product tests demonstrate a strong desire to test the product. This desire can intensify with each additional application and subsequent rejection, thereby further increasing the applicant's commitment. Repeated rejections resulting from repeated applications, driven by the desire for consistent behavior, further strengthen the commitment from one application to the next. It may also be a sign of "blind" consistency when an applicant continues to apply despite never being selected. Without much thought, the interested party simply continues to apply because they have done so several times before. Additionally, the desire increases with each rejection, as applicants realize that apparently many consumers are applying for the product tests and only a few have the privilege of being selected as testers. The higher commitment leads to further applications, even if applicants are rejected multiple times:

> "It's desirable to be a tester." *(male, 42)*,
>
> "Every rejection increases my desire be taken next time." *(male, 22)* and
>
> "I would still continue to make applications." *(female, 56)*.

Based on the theoretical arguments and the results of the exploratory qualitative survey, the following hypotheses are proposed:

> *H4a: The negative effect of a rejection in a product testing program among rejected applicants (compared to non-applicants) on purchase intention, mediated by an increase in perceived skepticism, is stronger after multiple rejections than after the first rejection.*

H4b: The positive effect of a rejection in a product testing program among rejected applicants (compared to non-applicants) on purchase intention, mediated by an increase in perceived commitment, is stronger after multiple rejections than after the first rejection.

H4c: The positive effect of a rejection in a product testing program among rejected applicants (compared to non-applicants) on the intention to spread negative word-of-mouth, mediated by an increase in perceived skepticism, is stronger after multiple rejections than after the first rejection.

H4d: The negative effect of a rejection in a product testing program among rejected applicants (compared to non-applicants) on the intention to spread negative word-of-mouth, mediated by an increase in perceived commitment, is stronger after multiple rejections than after the first rejection.

3.3.5 Summary of Hypotheses and Overview of the Research Model

Figure 3.4 provides an overview of the hypothesized relationships.

Hypothesis 1 can be derived from attribution theory and the findings of the exploratory qualitative study. A rejection in a product testing program increases the perceived skepticism of rejected applicants. This feeling of skepticism is based on the attribution process that is triggered as the rejected applicant seeks to understand the reason for the rejection. To protect their self-esteem, attribution bias may occur. The rejection is perceived by the applicant as externally caused, unstable, and uncontrollable. This self-serving attribution bias and the perceived instability lead to questioning the motives of the party responsible for the event. This can trigger skepticism as a negative emotion. The product test itself is called into question. As a result, after a rejection, an applicant may be skeptical as to whether the company truly intended to provide the promised test products, or whether the product test was merely used for advertising purposes or to collect applicant data. This perceived skepticism leads to a decrease in purchase intention and an increase in the intention to spread negative word-of-mouth.

Hypothesis 2 can be derived based on the commitment-consistency principle and the findings of the exploratory qualitative study. A rejection in a product testing program increases the perceived commitment of rejected applicants. This commitment arises with the initial application, in which the interested party makes

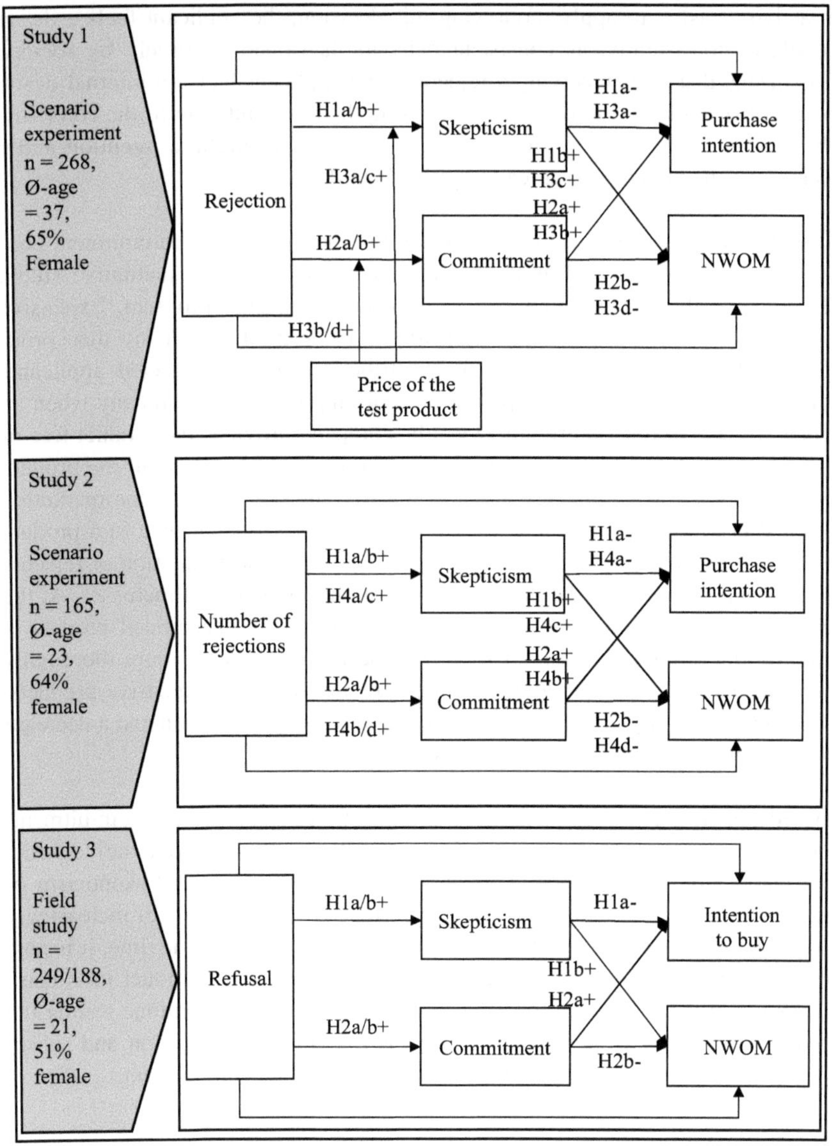

Fig. 3.4 Summary of the hypothesized relationships. *(Source:* Own illustration)

an active decision to apply. Following this decision, the applicant feels a desire to behave consistently, as consistent behavior is valued positively by society. This means that after receiving a rejection, the applicant feels an internal desire to act consistently and to continue expressing their commitment to the company. The increased commitment, in turn, leads to a higher purchase intention and a decrease in the intention to spread negative WOM.

Hypothesis 3 is derived from both attribution theory and the commitment-consistency principle, as well as the findings of the exploratory qualitative study. The price of the test products can vary depending on the program. Expensive test products that applicants can keep are more desirable for many than products worth only a few euros. In their attribution process, rejected applicants will assume that the costs of a product test are higher for the company when an expensive test product is offered, since the company provides the product free of charge. After receiving a rejection, they are more likely to question the product testing program, as companies seek to achieve a high return from the marketing tool and need to offset the costs. They will be more skeptical than in a product test with a less expensive product. As a result, the purchase intention of rejected applicants decreases and the intention to spread negative WOM increases. At the same time, applicants show higher commitment, as a higher-priced product is more desirable for consumers. They may research the product more thoroughly and consider their decision longer before applying for more expensive products. This higher commitment leads to an increase in purchase intention and a decrease in the intention to spread negative WOM.

Hypothesis 4 is also derived from both attribution theory and the commitment-consistency principle, as well as the findings of the exploratory qualitative study. The number of rejections has a positive effect on the perceived skepticism of rejected applicants. Product testers who are repeatedly rejected will increasingly question the product test and become more skeptical. At the same time, it is possible that applicants who repeatedly apply for a company's product tests demonstrate a strong desire for consistent behavior and wish to continue testing the product. This desire may intensify with each additional application and subsequent rejection, thereby further increasing the applicant's commitment.

Empirical Study 4

The following sections present the empirical investigation, which comprises a total of three studies. First, an overview of the studies (**Sect. 4.1**) and the hypotheses tested is provided. This is followed by a justification of the chosen research designs (**Sect. 4.2**), after which Study 1 (**Sect. 4.3**), Study 2 (**Sect. 4.4**), and finally Study 3 (**Sect. 4.5**) are explained.

4.1 Overview of the Studies

To test the hypotheses, two experimental studies and one field study were conducted. Figure 3.4 (Sect. 3.3.5) already provided a detailed overview of the three studies conducted. Study 1 experimentally analyzes the negative and positive behavioral consequences of rejections in the context of product testing programs, as well as the underlying psychological mechanisms. The study examines the extent to which rejected applicants experience skepticism and commitment, and how these variables affect their purchase intention and their intention to spread negative word-of-mouth. In addition, the moderating effect of the test product's price is tested. For this purpose, a scenario experiment with a total of 268 participants was conducted and analyzed using PROCESS. Building on Study 1, Study 2 tests the assumed effects of the number of rejections on customer behavior. This scenario experiment involved 165 participants and was also analyzed using

K. L. Küpper, *Negative and Positive Effects of Rejections in Online Product Testing Programs*, https://doi.org/10.1007/978-3-658-49277-9_4

PROCESS. The field study (Study 3) replicates the results in a real-world setting. Students had the opportunity to apply for a real product test of a unisex T-shirt with a university design. To reduce self-selection effects, the statistical matching approach and the difference-in-differences method are applied.

4.2 Justification of the Research Designs

The hypotheses are tested in the following by means of two experimental studies and one field study. This approach can be described as a **mixed-methods approach**. Leading scholars refer to mixed-methods when different data sources and design elements are used to uncover various perspectives. This approach aims to increase validity and to gain a broader understanding of the phenomenon under investigation (Kuckartz 2014, pp. 30 ff.). If the exploratory qualitative study from Sect. 3.1 is also taken into account, the requirements of those scholars who argue that qualitative data should also be collected and analyzed are met. The mixed-methods approach thus involves the combination of qualitative and quantitative data. Due to the preceding exploratory qualitative study, this case is referred to as a **sequential design**, in which the qualitative study precedes the quantitative studies (generalization design) (Kuckartz 2014, p. 77). The quantitative studies are conducted in this order to generalize the qualitative findings. This is achieved, among other things, by using a larger sample size than in the qualitative study (Kuckartz 2014, pp. 81 f.).

Since hypotheses were developed based on theory and the exploratory qualitative study, the scenario experiments—which are a type of laboratory experiment—and the field study are also referred to as **explanatory** studies. These studies serve to test the previously formulated hypotheses for validity. Döring and Bortz (2016, p. 194) define the aim of an experiment as follows: "The aim of an experiment [...] is the theory-based examination of the causal influence of one or more independent variables [...] on the manifestations of one or more dependent variables" (Döring/Botz 2016, p. 194). They use their quantitative data to test the previously postulated effects. Experimental studies are best suited to demonstrate causality, i.e., cause-and-effect relationships, between effects. For an explanatory study to allow causal inference, at least two groups must be formed and compared (experimental group vs. control group). In experimental studies, assignment to the two groups is carried out by randomization. This is also the case in the two scenario experiments described below. Thus, laboratory experiments generally exhibit high internal validity but limited external validity (Koschate 2008, p. 111; Schnell/Hill/Esser 2011, pp. 218 f.).

In contrast, the field study is considered a "quasi-experiment", as participants are not assigned to groups by randomization but instead self-select into one of the groups (Döring/Bortz 2016, p. 193; Schnell/Hill/Esser 2011, pp. 221 f.). The central problem of "quasi-experiments" is the resulting self-selection. Proper analyses must therefore account for these self-selection effects. A suitable method, which is applied in this work, is propensity score matching (Schnell/Hill/Esser 2011, p. 222). A field study is well suited to test the hypotheses, as it captures actual behavior as opposed to scenario experiments. Participants are not placed in an artificial situation that they are asked to imagine, but instead experience the situation directly. Such studies are therefore generally attributed higher external validity (Schnell/Hill/Esser 2011, p. 218).

By combining both qualitative and quantitative data, as well as laboratory and field studies, it can be assumed that, after conducting the studies, generalizable statements can be made about the effects of rejections in product testing programs.

4.3 Study 1—Consequences of Rejections and the Role of Product Price

This section first defines the study objective (**Sect. 4.3.1**). This is followed by a description of the study design (**Sect. 4.3.2**) and the implementation of the experiment (**Sect. 4.3.3**). Next, the recruitment and composition of the sample are presented (**Sect. 4.3.4**), and the operationalization of the variables is explained (**Sect. 4.3.5**). Finally, the results are presented (**Sect. 4.3.5**).

4.3.1 Study Objective

The initial exploratory qualitative survey and the theoretical foundations have generated initial insights into the perceptions and behavior of rejected applicants in online product testing programs. The aim of the following study is to test the psychologically assumed mechanisms and the behavior of rejected applicants in a first scenario experiment. Both the direct effects of a rejection in an online product testing program on purchase intention and the intention to spread negative word-of-mouth are examined, as well as the indirect effects on perceived skepticism and perceived commitment toward the rejecting company. In addition, by manipulating the price of the test product, its influence on the perceived skepticism and commitment of the rejected applicant is investigated.

4.3.2 Study Design

A scenario experiment conducted online was chosen as the study design. The scenario represents a fictitious situation into which participants were asked to immerse themselves (Eroglu 1987, p. 236). The present study employs an **experimental design with random group assignment**. This is characterized by the fact that the total group of participants is randomly assigned to one of the experimental groups. Thus, each participant experiences only one experimental condition (**between-subjects design**; Koschate-Fischer/Schandelmaier 2014, p. 802). Randomization ensures that personal characteristics have no effect on the dependent variables when assigning participants (Aaker et al. 2013, pp. 281 f.; Eifler/Leitgöb 2022, pp. 231 f.). Randomization therefore serves as a methodological control technique. The study employed a **design without pre-measurement**, meaning that the treatment group receives the stimulus—in this case, applicants receive a rejection—while the control group does not receive the stimulus (Kreis/Wildner/Kuß 2021, pp. 200 f.; Patry 1982, p. 25). In the present study, the control group does not apply for the product test, as they receive no information about the product test. Furthermore, a **factorial experimental design** was used. The independent variable "rejection" was manipulated at two levels, as was the independent variable "price." This results in a 2-x-2 design with a total of four experimental groups. The advantage of a factorial design is that the effect of each individual independent variable can be determined, as well as the interaction between the variables (Koschate 2008, pp. 113 ff.; Eifler/Leitgöb 2022, p. 235). The experimental design is illustrated in Fig. 4.1.

4.3.3 Implementation

The scenario experiment was programmed online using the SoSci Survey website and made available to participants via a link. Participants could access and complete the survey using a smartphone or computer. Randomization of participants was ensured through programming. All participants took part in the experiment voluntarily and without any incentives.

At the beginning of the experiment, participants were welcomed with a brief introductory text and informed that the study aimed to examine the effects of

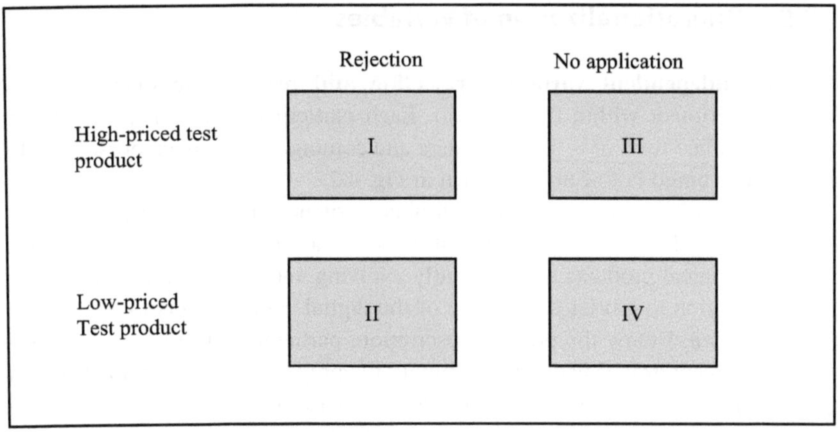

Fig. 4.1 Experimental design of scenario experiment 1. *(Source:* Own illustration)

product tests. Subsequently, each participant was presented with one of the four scenarios and asked to immerse themselves in the situation. After the scenario, questions regarding the dependent variables were presented, followed by questions on the mediator variables. Participants were also asked to assess the realism of the situation, and a manipulation check was conducted to ensure that the manipulation in the scenario was perceived. Finally, participants were asked to provide some demographic information about themselves.

4.3.4 Recruitment and Composition of the Sample

Participants were recruited using a procedure similar to that of Tokman, Davis, and Lemon (2007). Students in a bachelor's course were given age quotas according to which they recruited participants. In total, the sample consisted of 268 participants. The treatment group comprised 140 participants, and the control group 128 participants. The age of participants ranged from 16 to 70 years, with an average age of 37 years. 65% of participants were female, 35% male, and 0% diverse. Regarding educational background, 1% of participants reported having no educational qualification, 7% had a lower secondary school certificate, 26% an intermediate school certificate, 34% (specialized) university entrance qualification, and 32% a university degree.

4.3.5 Operationalization of Variables

The two **independent variables, rejection and price**, were operationalized in this experiment within the scenario. Each participant was asked to imagine searching online for a new digital camera and coming across an advertisement for the fictitious brand Foto-Star, as shown in Fig. 4.2.

A fictitious brand was chosen to eliminate potential bias due to prior experience with a real brand, and the digital camera was selected as the test product because technical products are constantly evolving and are of interest to all genders. In addition to a brief description of the digital camera, a photo of the camera was shown. Below the product description, participants in the product tester group (treatment group) had the opportunity to apply to test the camera. The non-applicant group (control group) could only purchase the camera and received no information about a possible product test. The treatment group received information on the next page about the product test procedure and was informed that they had received a rejection from the company after the application deadline. To manipulate the price, the price of the camera was also stated in the brief product description for all participants. In two of the four scenarios, a high product price of €599.99 was displayed, while in the other two scenarios, a low product price of €69.99 was shown.

The two **dependent variables**, purchase intention and negative WOM, were measured, following Kim et al. (2023, p. 444), by asking participants to indicate the probability in % (0% = very unlikely; 100% = very likely). Participants were asked to assess how likely they would be to purchase the product or to report predominantly negative things about Foto-Star. This allowed participants to specify very precisely their intention to purchase the test product and their intention to spread negative WOM. The dependent variables were measured with a single item, following the study by Bergkvist and Rossiter (2007), as the variables were formulated concretely. This approach can achieve validity comparable to that of multi-item operationalizations (Bergkvist/Rossiter 2007, pp. 182 f.; Mende/Bolton/Bitner 2013, p. 131).

The **mediator variables** skepticism and commitment, as psychological mechanisms, were each measured using seven-point Likert scales ranging from 1 = “strongly disagree” to 7 = “strongly agree.” Established multi-item scales were used. The items for the variable skepticism were adapted from Eggert, Steinhoff, and Garnefeld (2015, p. 217). Participants were asked, using three items, to indicate how skeptical the Foto-Star digital camera advertisement made them feel. The items for the variable commitment were adapted from Fullerton (2005,

Page 1:
Imagine you are surfing the Internet and looking for a new digital camera.
You find the following offer for a digital camera:

Foto-Star

Foto-Star full-frame digital camera

Experience the latest technology and further innovations in image processing!
For a price of **€599.99** you get the technology to capture unique moments the way you want!

Find out more

Buy now

Page 2:
You decide to apply as a product tester for the digital camera from Foto-Star:

Foto-Star

Apply now as a product tester and test exclusively!

This is how it works:

1. Apply
2. Receive your test product
3. Test the product
4. Write a review
5. Keep your product

You will receive a **rejection** after the application deadline.

Fig. 4.2 Scenario description for Scenario Experiment 1. (*Source:* Own illustration)

Table 4.1 Operationalization scenario experiment 1

Construct	Items
Purchase intention	I would be ...% likely to purchase the full-frame digital camera from Foto-Star.
Negative WOM	I am ...% likely to report predominantly negative things about Foto-Star.
Skepticism	The offer of the full-frame digital camera from Foto-Star makes me skeptical.
	The offer of the full-frame digital camera from Foto-Star makes me suspicious.
	The offer of the full-frame digital camera from Foto-Star arouses distrust in me.
Commitment	I feel emotionally connected to the Foto-Star brand.
	The Foto-Star brand is important to me.
	I can identify with the Foto-Star brand.

Source: Own illustration.

p. 1381). Here, participants were asked to indicate, using three statements, how connected they felt to the Foto-Star brand. The items for both variables were translated into German and adapted to the scenario. An overview of the operationalization of the scales is provided in Table 4.1.

4.3.6 Results

The following sections present the results of the study. First, the results of the manipulation and realism checks (**Sect. 4.3.6.1**) as well as the construct measurement (**Sect. 4.3.6.2**) are presented. Finally, the hypotheses are tested (**Sect. 4.3.6.3**).

4.3.6.1 Manipulation and Realism Check

First, it was checked whether the manipulation of the rejection was successful. For this purpose, participants were asked in the questionnaire whether they had received a rejection for the product test of the full-frame digital camera from Foto-Star. The treatment group, which received information about the product test and the subsequent rejection after the application phase in the scenario, differed significantly from the control group, which received no information about a product test. ($t(234.79) = -9.16$; $p < 0.01$; $M_{rejection} = 5.03$; $SD_{rejection} = 2.45$; $M_{no\ application} = 2.59$; $SD_{no\ application} = 1.84$); 1 = "strongly disagree," 7 = "strongly agree"). Thus, successful manipulation was ensured.

Next, it was checked whether the manipulation of the test product's price was successful. The price of the test product was stated in the brief product description in the scenario and was either €69.99 (low price) or €599.99 (high price). Here, too, the experimental groups with the high stated price differed significantly from those with the low stated price ($t(255.42) = -10.60$; $p < 0.01$; $M_{high} = 4.66$; $SD_{high} = 1.44$; $M_{low} = 2.71$; $SD_{low} = 1.56$; 1 = "strongly disagree," 7 = "strongly agree"). Therefore, the price manipulation was also successful in this case.

Additionally, a realism check was conducted to ensure that participants perceived the scenario as realistic. They were asked whether they could easily imagine themselves in the described situation. According to the realism check, the scenario was perceived as realistic and participants found it easy to imagine the situation ($M = 4.18$, $SD = 1.97$; 1 = "strongly disagree," 7 = "strongly agree").

4.3.6.2 Construct Measurement

Insights into the quality of the operationalization of the dependent variables are examined as part of construct measurement. The key criteria for assessment are the reliability and validity of the constructs. A widely used method for evaluating quality is **confirmatory factor analysis**. This method is used to examine the factor structure of the given indicators and subsequently to aggregate them into factors (Homburg/Giering 1996, p. 9).

To measure **construct reliability**, Cronbach's alpha (Cronbach 1951, p. 297) is frequently used. It measures the reliability of a group of indicators that load on a factor and indicates the internal consistency of the indicators (Homburg/Giering 1996, p. 8). The higher the alpha coefficient, the greater the reliability. A lower threshold of 0.7 is often adopted, following the recommendation of Nunnally (1987, p. 245). In addition, the average variance extracted is often analyzed, for which a high reliability value (< 0.5) is also desirable (Homburg/Giering 1996, p. 11). The average variance extracted indicates the proportion of variance of a construct in relation to the variance of measurement error (Fornell/Larcker 1981, pp. 45 f.).

In addition to assessing reliability, factor reliability and average variance extracted, together with factor loadings, can also be used to test convergent validity. If all indicators load sufficiently highly on a factor (factor loading < 0.7), they can be clearly assigned to the factor and are considered to have convergent validity (Homburg/Giering 1996, p. 8; Hulland 1999, p. 198). In addition to convergent validity, discriminant validity must also be assessed to ensure that **construct validity** is present. To determine discriminant validity, the square root of the average variance extracted is compared with the correlations of the other constructs. If this value is greater than the other correlations, discriminant validity is assumed (Fornell/Larcker 1981, p. 46).

The constructs of skepticism and commitment were examined using confirmatory factor analysis. As shown in Table 4.2, the construct reliability of the scales, with Cronbach's alpha values of 0.97 (skepticism) and 0.98 (commitment), exceeds the required threshold of 0.8. The average variance extracted is also above the threshold of 0.5, with values of 0.95 (skepticism) and 0.88 (commitment). Thus, the variables skepticism and commitment can be considered reliable. Convergent and discriminant validity for the variables skepticism and commitment were also assessed. The factor loadings, with at least 0.97 (skepticism) and 0.91 (commitment), surpass the threshold of 0.7, and the Fornell-Larcker criterion further confirms discriminant validity.

Table 4.2 Assessment of construct measurement scenario experiment 1

Construct Correlations							
Construct	M	SD	Factor Loading (> 0.7)[1]	Cronbach's α (> 0.7)[1]	AVE (> 0.5)[1]	Skepticism	Commitment
Purchase Intention	27.44	26.99					
Negative WOM	26.57	29.16					
Skepticism	4.12	2.04	0.973	0.97	0.95 (0.97)[2]		−0.08
	4.09	2.00	0.979				
	4.03	2.07	0.973				
Commitment	1.78	1.26	0.938	0.93	0.88 (0.94)[2]	−0.08	
	1.77	1.30	0.954				
	1.82	1.33	0.914				

M = Mean; SD = Standard Deviation; AVE = Average Variance Extracted
[1] Numbers in parentheses are threshold values.
[2] Numbers in parentheses are the square roots of the AVE.
Source: Own illustration.

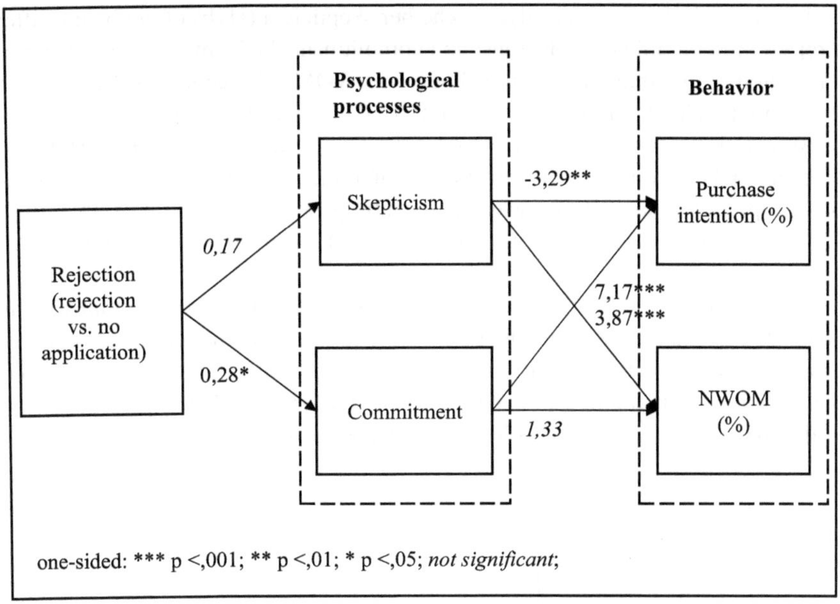

Fig. 4.3 Results of PROCESS Model 4, Scenario Experiment 1. (*Source:* Own illustration)

4.3.6.3 Hypothesis Testing

The PROCESS procedure (Hayes 2018) was used for hypothesis testing. First, Model 4 was applied to analyze the effects of rejection on purchase intention and the intention to spread negative WOM. In addition, the indirect effects via perceived skepticism and commitment were evaluated. An overview of the analysis using PROCESS Model 4 is presented in Fig. 4.3.

Using Model 4, the mediated effect of a rejection on the purchase intention of rejected applicants via skepticism (H1a) and commitment (H2a) was analyzed. The bootstrap method (5000 samples) yielded confidence intervals (CI) that excluded 0 for the indirect effect via commitment ($b=2.03$, $SE=1.09$, 90% $CI=[0.29, 3.86]$), but not for the indirect effect via skepticism ($b=-0.38$, $SE=0.81$, 90% $CI=[-1.77, 0.92]$). Thus, hypothesis H2a can be confirmed, but not hypothesis H1a. The direct effect of a rejection on the purchase intention of applicants was not significant ($t=-1.63$, $p=0.11$, 90% $CI=[-9.94, 0.08]$), nor was the total effect ($b=-3.29$, $p=0.32$, 90% $CI=[-8.74, 2.16]$).

In a second step, it was analyzed whether skepticism (H1b) of applicants after a rejection in an online product test and commitment (H2b) mediate the effect of a rejection on the intention to spread negative WOM. The generated CI included 0 for both indirect effects (skepticism: b=0.45, SE=0.98, 90% CI=[−1.06, 2.13]; commitment: b=0.38, SE=0.44, 90% CI=[−0.20, 1.18]). Thus, H1b and H2b cannot be confirmed. The direct effect of a rejection on the applicants' intention to spread negative WOM was significantly positive (t=3.02, p=0.003, 90% CI=[4.68, 15.96]), as was the total effect (b=11.15, p=0.002, 90% CI=[5.36, 16.94]).

Subsequently, a test of moderated mediation (Model 7, 5,000 samples) was conducted to examine whether the price of the test product moderates the hypothesized indirect effects of a rejection on the purchase intention of applicants and the intention to spread negative WOM (H3a, H3b, H3c, and H3d). An overview of the analysis using PROCESS Model 7 is shown in Fig. 4.4.

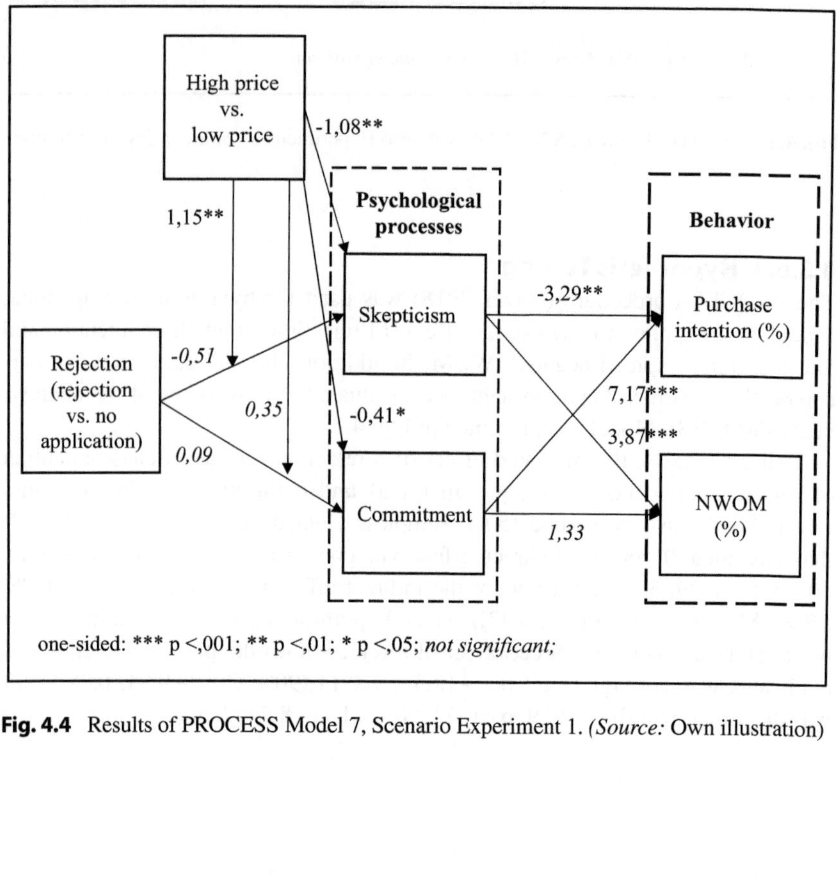

Fig. 4.4 Results of PROCESS Model 7, Scenario Experiment 1. (*Source:* Own illustration)

Supporting H3a, a significant indirect effect was found between rejection and a high product price on the purchase intention of applicants due to perceived skepticism ($b = -3.79$, $SE = 1.75$, 90% $CI = [-6.85, -1.12]$). These results indicate that the purchase intention of applicants, mediated by skepticism, decreases when the price of the test product is high (high price: $b = -2.12$, $SE = 1.18$, 90% $CI = [-4.15, -0.30]$). The indirect effect between rejection and a low product price on the purchase intention of rejected applicants, mediated by skepticism, is not significant (low price: $b = 1.67$, $SE = 1.21$, 90% $CI = [-0.21, 3.76]$). Contrary to hypothesis H3b, however, price has no effect on the indirect effect of rejection on the purchase intention of rejected applicants, mediated by perceived commitment ($b = 2.49$, $SE = 2.29$, 90% $CI = [-0.97, 6.57]$). The direct effect of a rejection on the purchase intention of rejected applicants is not significant ($t = -1.41$, $p = 0.17$, 90% $CI = [-0.99, 0.09]$), nor is the total effect at either price level (low price: $b = -5.19$, $SE = 5.18$, 90% $CI = [-13.77, 3.40]$; high price: $b = -1.97$, $SE = 4.15$, 90% $CI = [-8.85, 4.91]$).

In the next step, the effects on the dependent variable negative WOM were analyzed (H3c and H3d). A significant indirect effect of rejection and product price on the intention to spread negative WOM was found, mediated by skepticism ($b = 4.46$, $SE = 2.18$, 90% $CI = [1.27, 8.28]$) for a high product price. Thus, hypothesis H3c can be confirmed. These results indicate that the intention of rejected applicants to spread negative WOM, mediated by perceived skepticism, increases when the product price of the test product is high (high price: $b = 2.50$, $SE = 1.43$, 90% $CI = [0.37, 5.07]$). Again, no significant effect was found for a low product price (low price: $b = -1.96$, $SE = 1.44$, 90% $CI = [-4.44, 0.20]$). Price has no effect on the indirect effect of rejection on the intention to spread negative WOM, mediated by perceived commitment ($b = 0.46$, $SE = 0.70$, 90% $CI = [-0.36, 1.79]$). Thus, hypothesis H3d cannot be confirmed. However, price directly influences perceived skepticism ($t = -3.25$, $p = 0.001$, 90% $CI = [-1.63, -0.53]$) and perceived commitment ($t = -1.99$, $p = 0.05$, 90% $CI = [-0.74, -0.07]$). The direct effect of a rejection on the intention to spread negative WOM is significantly positive ($t = 3.02$, $p = 0.002$, 90% $CI = [4.68, 15.96]$), as is the total effect for high-priced products (low price: $b = 6.60$, $SE = 5.00$, 90% $CI = [-1.69, 14.89]$; high price: $b = 15.38$, $SE = 4.90$, 90% $CI = [7.26, 23.50]$).

4.4 Study 2—Consequences of Rejections and the Role of the Number of Rejections

The following sections first describe the study objective (**Sect. 4.4.1**), followed by the study design (**Sect. 4.4.2**), implementation (**Sect. 4.4.3**), recruitment and composition of the sample (**Sect. 4.4.4**), and operationalization of the variables (**Sect. 4.4.5**). Finally, the results of the study are explained (**Sect. 4.4.6**).

4.4.1 Study Objective

The hypothesized effects of a rejection on the perception and behavior of rejected applicants were examined for the first time in Study 1. It was found that, under certain conditions, both purchase intention and the intention to spread negative WOM increase after a rejection. These effects are mediated by perceived skepticism and commitment, and are partially moderated by price. In Study 2, these results are to be replicated using another scenario experiment, and the contextual factor of the number of rejections will be additionally investigated. This approach enhances the internal validity of the results and allows for the first-time testing of hypotheses H4a, H4b, H4c, and H4d. In this way, it becomes clear whether the number of rejections has an impact on purchase intention and the intention to spread negative WOM. Furthermore, it will be shown whether repeated rejections influence perceived skepticism and perceived commitment.

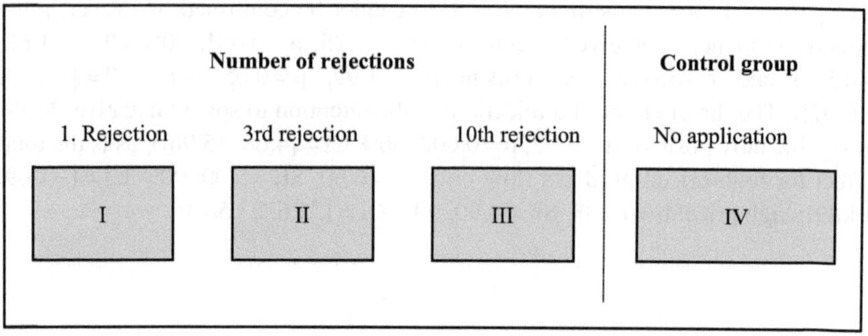

Fig. 4.5 Study design of scenario experiment 2. (*Source:* Own illustration)

4.4.2 Study Design

To analyze the influence of the number of previous rejections on the behavior and feelings of rejected applicants, a scenario experiment was again chosen. Study 2 also employs an **experimental design with random group assignment**. Thus, each participant is exposed to only one experimental condition (**between-subjects design**). A **design without pre-measurement** was selected for this study, meaning that the treatment group receives the stimulus—in this case, the applicants receive a rejection—while the control group does not receive the stimulus. In this case, the control group receives no information about the product test or the rejection. The experiment is a **unifactorial experimental design**. The independent variable, number of rejections, is manipulated at three levels, as shown in Fig. 4.5. This results in a 1-x-3 design plus a control group, with a total of three treatment groups and one control group (Koschate 2008, p. 113 ff.).

4.4.3 Implementation

The study was conducted at a total of three different universities in Germany. Students from the University of Wuppertal, the University of Rostock, and the University of Paderborn participated voluntarily and without incentives as part of lectures and during breaks between lectures. The students were informed that the experiment was part of a dissertation project focusing on product testing programs. The survey was provided to the students in printed form.

As in the first study, the students were instructed at the beginning of the survey to read the scenario carefully and to put themselves in the described situation. Subsequently, each participant was presented with one of the four scenarios. After the scenario, questions regarding the dependent variables—purchase intention and negative WOM—were asked, and the mediator variables skepticism and commitment were surveyed. Participants were also asked to assess the realism of the situation, and a manipulation check was conducted to ensure that the manipulation in the scenario was successful. Finally, participants were asked to provide information about their age, gender, and occupation.

The completed questionnaires were then reviewed and transferred into a digital format.

4.4.4 Recruitment and Composition of the Sample

The sample for this study consists of students. In total, the sample comprises 165 participants. Of these, 124 participants were in the treatment groups (first rejection: 37 participants; third rejection: 40 participants; tenth rejection: 47 participants) and 41 participants were in the control group. The age of the participants ranged from 16 to 34 years, with an average age of 23 years. 63% of the participants were female, 37% male, and 0% diverse. Regarding educational background, 1% of participants reported having no educational qualification, 2% had a lower secondary school certificate, 0% had an intermediate school certificate, 35% had a (subject-specific) university entrance qualification, and 62% had a university degree.

4.4.5 Operationalization of Variables

The independent variable "rejection" and the contextual factor "number of rejections" were operationalized in this experiment within the scenario. As in Study 1, each participant was asked to imagine searching online for a new digital camera and coming across an advertisement for the fictitious brand Elektro Star. The same description and presentation of the digital camera were used as in Study 1. As before, under the camera description, participants in the product tester group (treatment group) had the opportunity to apply to test this camera. The non-applicant group (control group) could only purchase the camera and did not receive any information about a potential product test. On the following page, the treatment group was informed that this was their first, third, or already their tenth application to the company for a product test, and that they had never been selected as a product tester. These frequencies were adopted from the exploratory interview study, where they were mentioned by applicants. Again, the participants received a rejection for the product test of the full-frame digital camera from Elektro Star.

The dependent variable purchase intention was measured in this study using three items on a seven-point Likert scale, ranging from 1 = "strongly disagree" to 7 = "strongly agree." The variables were adapted from Netemeyer, Maxham III, and Pullig (2005, p. 141). Negative WOM was again measured, following Kim et al. (2023, p. 444), by asking for the probability in % (0% = very unlikely; 100% = very likely).

Table 4.3 Operationalization of scenario experiment 2

Construct	Items
Purchase Intention	I am seriously considering purchasing the full-frame digital camera from Elektro Star.
	I am considering becoming a customer of Elektro Star.
	I can easily imagine buying the full-frame digital camera from Elektro Star.
Negative WOM	With a probability of ... %, I will mostly report negative things about Elektro Star.
Skepticism	The offer of the full-frame digital camera from Elektro Star makes me skeptical.
	The offer of the full-frame digital camera from Elektro Star makes me suspicious.
	The offer of the full-frame digital camera from Elektro Star arouses distrust in me.
Commitment	I feel emotionally connected to the Elektro Star brand.
	The Elektro Star brand is important to me.
	I can identify with the Elektro Star brand.

Source: Own illustration.

The mediator variables skepticism and commitment as psychological mechanisms were, as in Study 1, each measured on seven-point Likert scales ranging from 1 = "strongly disagree" to 7 = "strongly agree." The same items for the variable skepticism from Eggert, Steinhoff, and Garnefeld (2015, p. 217) and for the variable commitment from Fullerton (2005, p. 1381) were adapted (Table 4.1, Sect. 4.3.5).

An overview of the operationalization of the scales is provided in Table 4.3.

4.4.6 Results

The following sections present the results of the study. First, the results of the manipulation and reality checks (**Sect. 4.4.6.1**) and the construct measurement (**Sect. 4.4.6.2**) are presented. Finally, the hypotheses are tested (**Sect. 4.4.6.3**).

4.4.6.1 Manipulation and Reality Check

As in Study 1, it was first checked whether the manipulation of the rejection was successful. Since the number of rejections was also manipulated in this scenario, participants were asked in the questionnaire whether they had applied to test the full-frame digital camera. The treatment groups, who received information about the product test and the first, third, or tenth rejection after the application phase, differed significantly from the control group, who received no information about a product test ($t(162) = 17.33$; $p < 0.001$; $M_{rejections} = 6.35$; $SD_{rejections} = 1.54$; $M_{no\ application} = 1.63$; $SD_{no\ application} = 1.35$); 1 = "strongly disagree", 7 = "strongly agree"). Thus, successful manipulation of the rejection was ensured.

Next, it was checked whether the number of rejections was perceived. The number of rejections received (first, third, or tenth) was communicated to the participants in the treatment groups on the second page of the scenario. Here, too, the individual treatment groups differed significantly from each other. The participants successfully indicated whether they had received their first rejection ($t(92.66) = -20.01$; $p < 0.01$; $M_{first\ rejection} = 6.65$; $SD_{first\ rejection} = 1.13$; $M_{third\ \&\ tenth\ rejection} = 1.59$; $SD_{third\ \&\ tenth\ rejection} = 1.54$), their third rejection ($t(52.90) = -12.87$; $p < 0.001$; $M_{third\ rejection} = 6.05$; $SD_{third\ rejection} = 1.41$; $M_{first\ \&\ tenth\ rejection} = 1.41$; $SD_{first\ \&\ tenth\ rejection} = 1.27$) or their tenth rejection ($t(68.55) = -15.13$;

Table 4.4 Assessment of construct measurement scenario experiment 2

Construct Correlations								
Construct	M	SD	Factor Loading (> 0.7)[1]	Cronbach's α (> 0.7)[1]	AVE (> 0.5)[1]	Purchase Intention	Skepticism	Commitment
Purchase Intention	2.96	1.67	0.96	0.95	0.90 (0.95)[2]		−0.20	0.53
	2.97	1.62	0.94					
	2.88	1.63	0.95					
Negative WOM	30.27	26.95						
Skepticism	3.97	1.69	0.92	0.92	0.88 (0.94)[2]			0.11
	3.82	1.74	0.95			−0.20		
	3.82	1.86	0.94					
Commitment	1.99	1.35	0.94	0.92	0.86 (0.93)[2]		0.11	
	1.95	1.38	0.92			0.531		
	1.96	1.31	0.92					

M = Mean; SD = Standard deviation; AVE = average variance extracted
[1] The numbers in parentheses are the threshold values.
[2] The numbers in parentheses are the square roots of the AVE.
Source: Own illustration.

$p < 0.001$; $M_{\text{tenth rejection}} = 6.22$; $SD_{\text{tenth rejection}} = 1.39$; $M_{\text{first \& third rejection}} = 1.39$; $SD_{\text{first \& third rejection}} = 1.24$; 1 = "strongly disagree", 7 = "strongly agree").

Additionally, a reality check was conducted to ensure that participants perceived the scenario as realistic. They were asked whether they could easily imagine themselves in the described situation. According to the reality check, the scenario was perceived as realistic and participants found it easy to imagine the situation (M = 4.59, SD = 1.83; 1 = "strongly disagree", 7 = "strongly agree").

4.4.6.2 Construct Measurement

The constructs purchase intention, skepticism, and commitment were examined using confirmatory factor analysis. As shown in Table 4.4 shows that the construct reliability of the scales, with Cronbach's alpha values of 0.95 (purchase intention), 0.92 (skepticism), and 0.92 (commitment), exceeds the required threshold of 0.7. The average variance extracted is also above the threshold of 0.5, with values of 0.90 (purchase intention), 0.88 (skepticism), and 0.86 (commitment). Thus, the variables purchase intention, skepticism, and commitment can be considered reliable. Convergent and discriminant validity for the variables purchase intention, skepticism, and commitment were also assessed. The factor

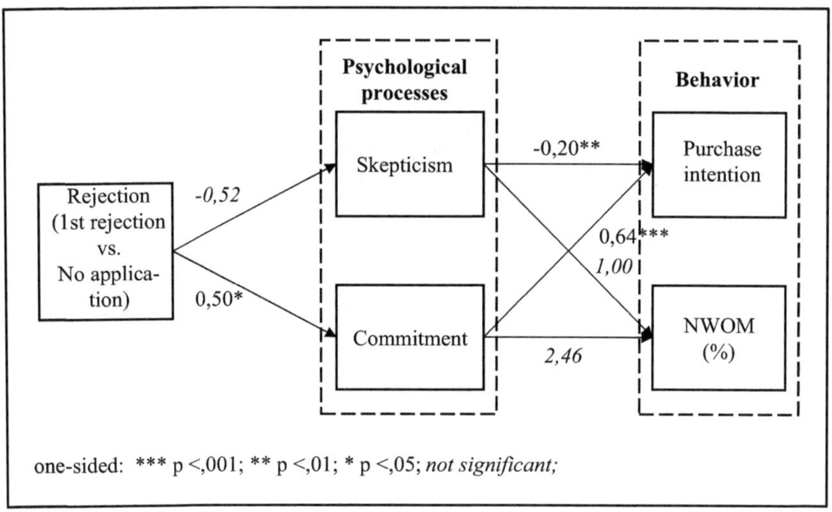

Fig. 4.6 Results of PROCESS Model 4, Scenario Experiment 2. (*Source:* Own illustration)

loadings, with at least 0.94 (purchase intention), 0.92 (skepticism), and 0.92 (commitment), exceed the threshold of 0.7, and the Fornell-Larcker criterion also confirms discriminant validity.

4.4.6.3 Hypothesis Testing

To analyze the impact of the number of rejections on perceived skepticism and commitment, and the resulting influence on purchase intention and negative WOM intention among rejected applicants, the PROCESS procedure (Hayes 2008) was used again. First, the results of Study 1 were replicated by analyzing the effects of a rejection on the purchase intention of the rejected applicant and the intention to engage in negative WOM, under the influence of perceived skepticism and commitment (H1 and H2). An overview of the analysis using PROCESS Model 4 (5000 samples) is shown in Fig. 4.6.

Model 4 was used to analyze the mediated effect of a rejection on the purchase intention of rejected applicants via skepticism (H1a) and commitment (H2a). The bootstrap procedure yielded confidence intervals (CI) that excluded 0 for the indirect effect via commitment ($b=0.32$, $SE=0.17$, 90% CI=[0.03, 0.60]), but not for the indirect effect via skepticism ($b=0.10$, $SE=0.10$, 90% CI=[−0.03, 0.27]). Thus, as in Study 1, hypothesis H2a can be confirmed, whereas hypothesis H1a cannot be confirmed. The direct effect of a rejection on applicants' purchase intention was not significant ($t=0.47$, $p=0.13$, 90% CI=[−0.04, 0.98]), but the total effect was significantly positive ($b=0.89$, $p=0.09$, 90% CI=[0.34, 1.45]).

In a second step, it was analyzed whether applicants' skepticism (H1b) after a rejection in an online product test and commitment (H2b) mediate the effect of a rejection on the intention to spread negative WOM. The generated CI included 0 for both indirect effects (skepticism $b=-0.46$, $SE=0.94$, 90% CI=[−2.30, 0.07]; commitment $b=1.19$, $SE=1.193$, 90% CI=[−0.38, 5.54]). As in Study 1, hypotheses H1b and H2b cannot be confirmed. The direct effect of a rejection on applicants' intention to spread negative WOM was not significant ($t=1.28$, $p=0.21$, 90% CI=[−1.93, 14.65]), nor was the total effect ($b=7.10$, $p=0.14$, 90% CI=[−0.87, 15.06]).

To test H4a, H4b, H4c, and H4d, dummy coding was used (Henseler/Fassott 2010, p. 726), in which the categorical independent variable was converted into several binary variables. The group with the first rejection was chosen as the reference category to examine differences between the various frequencies of rejection (first, third, and tenth rejection). An overview of the analysis using PROCESS Model 4 (5000 samples) is shown in Fig. 4.7.

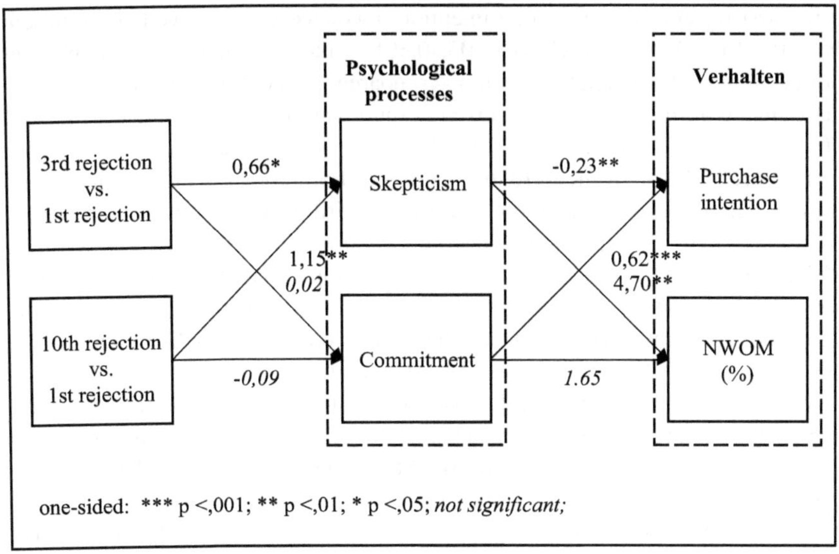

Fig. 4.7 Results of PROCESS Model 4, Scenario Experiment 2 with dummy coding. (*Source:* Own illustration)

The effect of the third rejection (compared to the first rejection) and perceived skepticism is significantly positive (b=0.66, p=0.07), as is the effect of the tenth rejection (compared to the first rejection) and perceived skepticism (b=1.15, p<0.05). In the analysis of purchase intentions, a significantly negative indirect effect of the third rejection (compared to the first rejection) on purchase intention is observed. This effect is mediated by perceived skepticism (b=−0.15, SE=0.11, 90% CI=[−0.35, −0.01]). Similarly, the indirect effect of the tenth rejection (compared to the first rejection) on purchase intention, mediated by perceived skepticism, is significantly negative (b=−0.27, SE=0.13, 90% CI=[−0.51, −0.08]). This confirms hypothesis H4a.

The effect of the third rejection (compared to the first rejection) and perceived commitment is not significant (b=0.02, p=0.94), nor is the effect of the tenth rejection (compared to the first rejection) and perceived commitment (b=−0.09, p=0.75). There is no significant indirect effect of the third rejection (compared to the first rejection) on purchase intention, mediated by perceived commitment ($b = 0.01$, $SE = 0.18$, 90% $CI = [-0.03, 0.30]$). Likewise, there is no significant indirect effect of the tenth rejection (compared to the first rejection) on purchase intention, mediated by perceived commitment ($b = -0.06$, $SE = 0.18$, 90% $CI = [-0.35, 0.23]$). Thus, hypothesis H4b cannot be confirmed.

The direct effects of the third and tenth rejection (compared to the first rejection) on purchase intention are not significant (third rejection: $t = -0.54$, $p = 0.59$, 90% $CI = [-0.67, 0.34]$; tenth rejection: $t = -0.74$, $p = 0.46$, 90% $CI = [-0.72, 0.28]$). The total effect of the third rejection (compared to the first rejection) on purchase intention is not significant ($b = -0.31$, $SE = 0.36$, 90% $CI = [-0.90, 0.28]$), nor is the total effect of the tenth rejection (compared to the first rejection) ($b = -0.55$, $SE = 0.34$, 90% $CI = [-1.12, 0.02]$).

With regard to the effects on the intention to spread negative WOM, a significant positive indirect effect of the third rejection (compared to the first rejection) on the intention to spread negative WOM, mediated by perceived skepticism, was found ($b = 3.23$, $SE = 2.08$, 90% $CI = [0.41, 7.05]$). The indirect effect of the tenth rejection (compared to the first rejection) on the intention to spread negative WOM, mediated by perceived skepticism, is also significantly positive ($b = 5.52$, $SE = 2.46$, 90% $CI = [1.89, 10.02]$). This confirms hypothesis H4c. There is no significant indirect effect of a third or tenth rejection (compared to the first rejection) on the intention to spread negative WOM, mediated by perceived commitment (third rejection: $b = 0.03$, $SE = 0.64$, 90% $CI = [-1.04, 1.03]$; tenth rejection: $b = -0.16$, $SE = 0.68$, 90% $CI = [-1.45, 0.69]$). Thus, hypothesis H4d cannot be confirmed.

The direct effect of the third rejection (compared to the first rejection) on the intention to spread negative WOM is significantly positive ($t = 1.72$, $p = 0.08$, 90% $CI = [0.35, 19.78]$), as is the direct effect of the tenth rejection (compared to the first rejection) on the intention to spread negative WOM, which is also significantly positive ($t = 2.36$, $p < 0.05$, 90% $CI = [4.11, 23.45]$). The total effect of the third rejection (compared to the first rejection) on the intention to spread negative WOM is significantly positive ($b = 13.32$, $SE = 5.99$, 90% $CI = [3.38, 23.25]$). The total effect of the tenth rejection (compared to the first rejection) on the intention to spread negative WOM is likewise significantly positive ($b = 19.14$, $SE = 5.77$, 90% $CI = [9.57, 28.71]$).

4.5 Study 3—Analysis of the Consequences of Rejections Using a Field Study

The following sections first describe the study objective (**Sect. 4.5.1**), followed by the study design (**Sect. 4.5.2**), implementation (**Sect. 4.5.3**), recruitment and composition of the sample (**Sect. 4.5.4**), and operationalization of the variables (**Sect. 4.5.5**). Finally, the results of the study are explained (**Sect. 4.5.6**).

4.5.1 Study Objective

In Study 3, real data collected in cooperation with the Uni-Shop of the University of Wuppertal are used to replicate the results from the previous studies and to increase external validity. The scenario experiments are meaningfully complemented by the field study, as real and observable behavior is analyzed. Thus, the conceptual model is tested using real field data. The study investigates in the field how a rejection in a product testing program affects purchase intention and the intention to spread negative WOM after a rejection in a product test (H1 and H2). Beyond the original conceptual model, a post-hoc analysis examines the effects of a rejection in a product testing program on the engagement of rejected applicants.

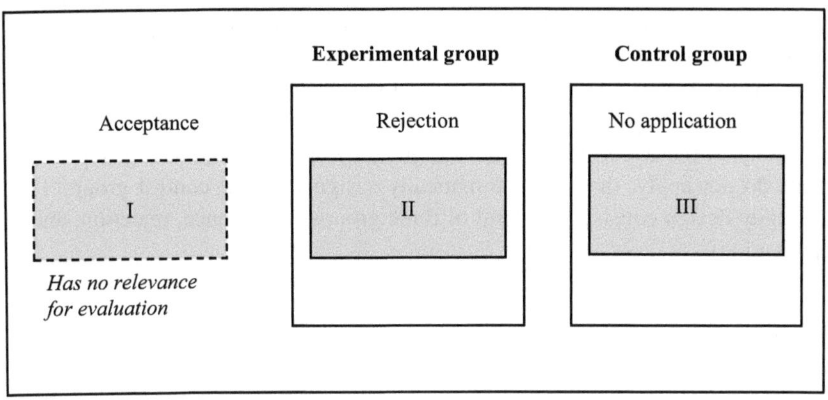

Fig. 4.8 Study design of the field study. (*Source:* Own illustration)

4.5.2 Study Design

To analyze the influence of the number of previous rejections on the behavior and feelings of rejected applicants in a real situation, a field study was chosen as the study design for the third study. Since random assignment of participants was not possible in this study, there was a risk that the internal validity of the study could be affected by confounding variables. This type of investigation is called a "**quasi-experiment**" (Campbell/Stanley 1963, p. 34; Eid/Gollwitzer/Schmitt 2017, pp. 92 f.; Schnell/Hill/Esser 2011, p. 222). The students independently decided, by voluntarily applying, whether they would be eligible for the experimental group or belong to the control group. In this case, internal validity was ensured by examining the participants before the experimental stimulus and identifying and controlling for possible confounding variables. This ensures control over the measurements (Eid/Gollwitzer/Schmitt 2017, pp. 92 f.). According to the classification by Döring (2023, p. 185), this is a **within-subjects design** due to the repeated measurements. The same group of students was surveyed first at the beginning of the semester, before the product test, and then again at the end of the semester, after the product test. An advantage of a within-subjects design is the ability to separately estimate the differences between individual participants and the experimental conditions (Koschate 2008, pp. 113 ff.).

An overview of the design is shown in Fig. 4.8.

For the first time in this study, the acceptance group is included, as it is automatically formed during the implementation of the product test. Although this group is not relevant for the later analysis, it is possible that participants are randomly assigned to the acceptance group after actively applying. Therefore, participants first decide with their application whether they can be selected for the experimental group, before being randomly assigned during the course of the study to the experimental group (rejection) or the acceptance group. If students do not apply, they are automatically assigned to the control group. Thus, the study design consists of a total of three groups (acceptance, rejection, and no application).

4.5.3 Implementation

To validate the previous results in practice, an online product test as well as pre- and post-test surveys were designed and conducted. The entire field study can be divided into three periods, as shown in Fig. 4.9.

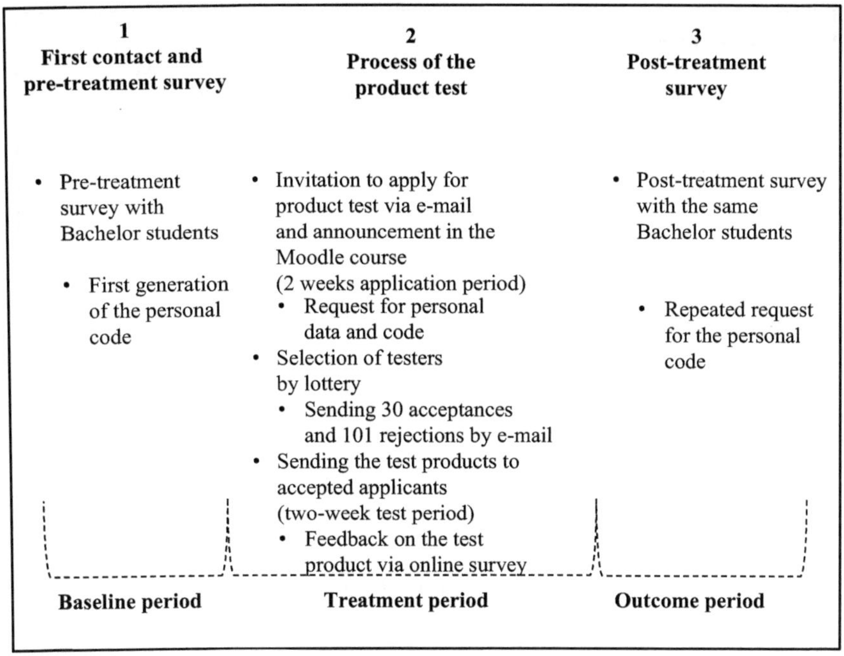

Fig. 4.9 Process of the field study. (*Source:* Own illustration)

During the **baseline period**, a dedicated product test was designed in collaboration with the university shop at the University of Wuppertal. The university shop sells products with the university logo, such as clothing, office supplies, and accessories. At the time of planning, the shop had launched a new fashion collection, from which a unisex T-shirt was selected as the test product. The T-shirt was mint green and featured the university logo. It was available in sizes XS-XXL, ensuring that almost all students could find their size. The regular price of the T-shirt was €17.90. For the purposes of the study, the university shop provided a total of 30 T-shirts free of charge as test products. Before the product test was announced and conducted, a marketing bachelor course at the University of Wuppertal, consisting of students at the beginning of their bachelor studies, was selected as participants for the study. As part of the marketing course, an initial survey (**pre-treatment survey**) was conducted during the introductory session at the start of the semester. Since the entire module was held online due to the COVID-19 pandemic, the introductory session also took place virtually via

Creation of the personal code:
In the following, we ask you to create a personal code and enter it in the input fields. The questions should help you to remember your personal combination later.

What is the first letter of your first name?	Please use your first name as it appears on your ID. Example: Max= M
What are the last two digits of your year of birth?	For a single-digit number, please use a leading 0. Example: 1999= 99
What is the first letter of your surname?	If you have changed your surname, please use your maiden name. Example: Mustermann= M
What day were you born?	For single-digit numbers, please use a leading 0. Example: January 01= 01
What is the first letter of your gender?	Please select W for female, M for male or D for diverse. Example: male= M
Your personal code:	

Fig. 4.10 Creation of the personal code. (*Source:* Own illustration)

Zoom. Students received the link to the survey, which had been programmed in advance using SoSci, via Zoom. Time was allocated during the lecture for students to complete the survey at their own pace. After the session, the survey link was also posted on the course page in Moodle and emailed to all enrolled students to reach those who had missed the introductory session. In the first survey, students were asked, among other things, about their attitudes toward product tests as well as the university shop and its products. In the online questionnaire, students provided information about their knowledge of the university shop and its products, their purchase intentions regarding university shop products, and their previous experiences with product tests.

To capture students' behavior and changes in attitudes, a scheme for an individual code was developed, which was created and entered by each student at the beginning of the survey. The process of creating and entering the code is illustrated in Fig. 4.10.

The first character of the code was the first letter of the first name, the second and third characters were the last two digits of the year of birth, the fourth character was the first letter of the last name, the fifth and sixth characters were the day of birth, and the seventh character was the gender, abbreviated as M, W, or D. In this way, each student generated an individual code, and every completed questionnaire began with this code. The code was based on stable personal characteristics to ensure that each student would still have the same code as at the start of the study, even after several weeks.

At the beginning of the **treatment period**, students in the bachelor module were **invited** to apply for the university shop product test. An announcement was created that both depicted the test product and explained the entire product test process. The announcement for the application period, including the advertisement, was sent to students by email and posted in the digital Moodle course. Students could apply online via a survey link, which was again programmed in advance using SoSci, and were required to enter their individual code as part of the application. They were also asked to provide some demographic information, such as age, gender, and nationality. In addition, applicants were asked to specify their desired T-shirt size and indicate whether they had previously purchased products from the university shop and, if so, which ones. Students had two weeks to apply for the product test. A total of 131 students applied. After the application period ended, 30 product testers were selected by **random draw** from all applicants. The **acceptance or rejection notifications** were sent to applicants by email.

The 30 selected product testers were congratulated and informed about the next steps. The remaining 101 applicants received a rejection email at the same time. From the time of notification, the product testers had one week to complete another short questionnaire. Via an online link to a brief survey programmed in SoSci, the product testers could reconfirm their desired T-shirt size and provide the address to which the T-shirt should be sent. During this week, the product testers were reminded twice by email to complete the survey. Afterwards, the **test products** were packaged and **sent** to the selected product testers.

The test period lasted two weeks, during which the product testers tried out the T-shirt. They were then asked to evaluate the product in an online questionnaire programmed in SoSci. The link to the questionnaire was sent to the product testers by email and included in their product tester package. At the beginning of the questionnaire, testers were asked to provide a 2–3 sentence overall assessment of the T-shirt. The test product was then evaluated based on characteristics such as wearing comfort, appearance, feel, quality, and fit. In addition, testers were asked to compare the T-shirt with other purchased T-shirts and to indicate the total wearing time. Finally, testers were asked to provide demographic information on age, gender, and nationality. Again, the selected product testers were reminded several times by email to complete the evaluation form. As part of the evaluation form, testers were again asked to enter their personal code. After the test phase, the product test and thus the treatment period were concluded.

In the final phase of the study, the **outcome period**, students in the bachelor course were again surveyed as part of a **post-treatment survey**. For this purpose, students were provided with the link to the survey, programmed in SoSci, during the last lecture of the semester and given time to complete it. After the session, the link was again posted in the Moodle course and emailed to all students to reach those who could not attend the session. To capture students' attitudes and changes in perception and behavior, the same questionnaire was used in the post-treatment survey as in the pre-treatment survey. Here, too, the individual code was requested in order to combine the data from the post-treatment survey with those from the pre-treatment survey and to determine whether the respective student had applied for the product test during the treatment period and whether they had been rejected or not. Using these individual codes, it was possible to precisely analyze changes in the behavior and attitudes of applicants as a result of being rejected from the product test.

4.5.4 Recruitment and Composition of the Sample

The participants were students enrolled in a bachelor's level marketing module at the University of Wuppertal, which was conducted entirely online due to the COVID-19 pandemic. The students were at the beginning of their studies and all were registered in a Moodle course where all lecture materials were uploaded and information about the module was provided. Every student enrolled in the course thus had the opportunity to voluntarily participate in the pre- and post-treatment surveys, either live during the lecture via Zoom or afterwards via the link provided in Moodle, without any incentive. The announcement and the link to apply for the product test were also distributed via Moodle and by email to all enrolled students.

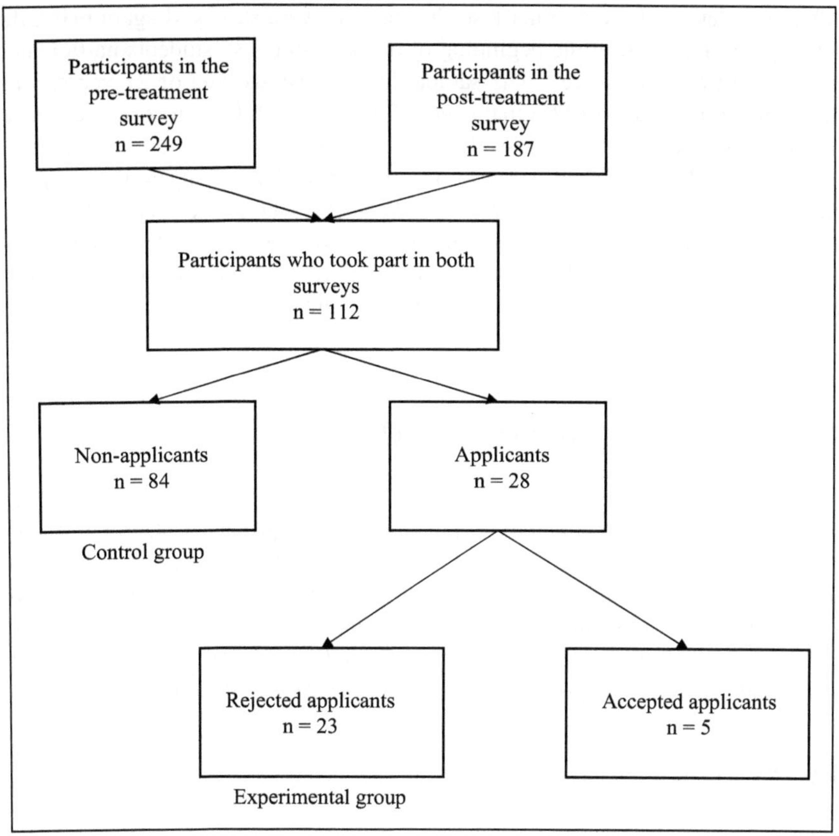

Fig. 4.11 Distribution of participants. (*Source:* Own illustration)

Figure 4.11 shows the distribution of students across the different groups. In addition, the figure indicates which groups were compared in the subsequent analysis.

A total of 249 students participated in the pre-treatment survey. The sample had an average age of 21 years, and 51% of the participants were female (49% male). After the pre-treatment survey, the product test was announced. All students in the module had the opportunity to voluntarily apply for the product test.

After completion of the product test, the students were surveyed again using the same questionnaire as at the beginning of the semester. 187 students participated in the post-treatment survey. The sample had an average age of 21 years, with 52% female participants (47% male and 1% non-binary). In analyzing the effects of rejection from the product test, the focus was initially placed on those participants who took part in both surveys, in order to analyze changes in perception and behavior. Within this subsample of 112 students who participated in both surveys, 84 students did not apply for the product test and 28 students did apply. Of these 28 applicants, 23 were rejected and 5 were selected as product testers. In the analysis, the rejected applicants (experimental group) are compared with those who did not apply (control group).

4.5.5 Operationalization of Variables

The operationalization of the independent variable "rejection" in this case was based on the students' voluntary application for the product test. For this purpose, a graphic was created to inform students about the product test and explain the procedure. The graphic also depicted the T-shirt as the test product and provided the link to apply. Students then had the opportunity to apply for the product test, and 30 product testers were selected at random. Assignment to the acceptance group or rejection group (experimental group) was therefore random. The

Table 4.5 Operationalization of the field study

Construct	Items
Purchase intention	I am seriously considering buying a product from the university shop.
	I am considering buying a product from the university shop.
	I can easily imagine buying a product from the university shop.
Negative WOM	With a probability of … %, I will speak negatively about the university shop of the University of Wuppertal to others.
Skepticism	Product testing programs make me skeptical.
	Product testing programs make me suspicious.
	Product testing programs arouse distrust in me.
Commitment	I feel connected to the university shop.
	The university shop is important to me.
	I can identify with the university shop.

Source: Own illustration.

remaining students who did not wish to apply for the product test were automatically assigned to the control group (see Fig. 4.11).

The dependent variable purchase intention was again measured in this study using three items on a seven-point Likert scale ranging from 1 = "strongly disagree" to 7 = "strongly agree." The variables were adapted from Netemeyer, Maxham III, and Pullig (2005, p. 141). Negative WOM was again measured by asking for the probability in %, following Kim et al. (2023, p. 444) (0% = very unlikely; 100% = very likely).

The mediator variables skepticism and commitment as psychological mechanisms were, as in Studies 1 and 2, each measured on seven-point Likert scales ranging from 1 = "strongly disagree" to 7 = "strongly agree." The same items for the variable skepticism were adapted from Eggert, Steinhoff, and Garnefeld (2015, p. 217), and the same items for the variable commitment were adapted from Fullerton (2005). Table 4.5 provides an overview of the constructs used and their items.

4.5.6 Results

The following sections first explain the construct measurement (**Sect. 4.5.6.1**), before presenting the propensity score matching (**Sect. 4.5.6.2**) and the difference-in-differences estimation (**Sect. 4.5.6.3**). The hypotheses are then tested (**Sect. 4.5.6.4**), and finally, a post-hoc analysis is conducted (**Sect. 4.5.6.5**).

4.5.6.1 Construct Measurement

The constructs purchase intention, skepticism, and commitment were examined using confirmatory factor analysis. First, the constructs from the pre-treatment survey were analyzed. As shown in Table 4.6, the construct reliability of the scales, with Cronbach's alpha values of 0.92 (purchase intention), 0.94 (skepticism), and 0.92 (commitment), exceeds the required threshold of 0.7. The average variance extracted is also above the threshold of 0.5, with values of 0.87 (purchase intention), 0.86 (skepticism), and 0.90 (commitment). Thus, the variables purchase intention, skepticism, and commitment can be considered reliable. Convergent and discriminant validity for the variables purchase intention, skepticism, and commitment was also assessed. The factor loadings, with at least 0.91 (purchase intention), 0.94 (skepticism), and 0.91 (commitment), exceed the threshold of 0.7, and the Fornell-Larcker criterion also confirms discriminant validity.

Subsequently, the same analysis was conducted for the constructs from the post-treatment survey. Construct reliability, with Cronbach's alpha values of

Table 4.6 Validation of construct measurement in the field study

Construct Correlations								
Construct	M	SE	Factor Loading (> 0.7)[1]	Cronbach's α (> 0.7)[1]	AVE (> 0.5)[1]	Purchase Intention	Skepticism	Commitment
	Pre-Treatment Survey							
Purchase Intention	2.52	1.67	0.94	0.92	0.87 (0.93)[2]		0.02	0.58
	3.18	1.79	0.94					
	3.39	1.86	0.91					
Negative WOM	11.81	18.49						
Skepticism	3.59	1.78	0.94	0.94	0.86 (0.93)[2]	0.02		0.02
	3.35	1.67	0.95					
	3.37	1.78	0.95					
Commitment	2.17	1.51	0.91	0.92	0.90 (0.95)[2]	0.58	0.02	
	1.78	1.24	0.95					
	2.0	1.34	0.93					
	Post-Treatment Survey							
Purchase Intention	2.71	1.67	0.95	0.94	0.87 (0.93)[2]		−0.01	0.60
	3.18	1.81	0.96					
	3.56	1.93	0.94					
Negative WOM	9.87	16.97						

(Fortsetzung)

Table 4.6 (Fortsetzung)

Construct Correlations								
Construct	M	SE	Factor Loading (> 0.7)[1]	Cronbach's α (> 0.7)[1]	AVE (> 0.5)[1]	Purchase Intention	Skepticism	Commitment
Skepticism	3.28	1.61	0.96	0.95	0.91 (0.95)[2]	−0.01		0.02
	3.13	1.52	0.96					
	3.08	1.59	0.95					
Commitment	2.53	1.60	0.94	0.93	0.88 (0.94)[2]	0.60	0.02	
	2.07	1.35	0.93					
	2.43	1.56	0.94					

M = Mean; SE = Standard deviation; DEV = average recorded variance
[1] The numbers in parentheses are the threshold values.
[2] The numbers in parentheses are the square roots of the DEV.
Source: Own illustration.

0.94 (purchase intention), 0.95 (skepticism), and 0.93 (commitment), exceeds the required threshold of 0.7. The average variance extracted is also above the threshold of 0.5, with values of 0.87 (purchase intention), 0.91 (skepticism), and 0.88 (commitment). Thus, the variables purchase intention, skepticism, and commitment can be considered reliable. Convergent and discriminant validity for the variables purchase intention, skepticism, and commitment was also assessed. The factor loadings, with at least 0.94 (purchase intention), 0.95 (skepticism), and 0.93 (commitment), exceed the threshold of 0.7, and the Fornell-Larcker criterion also confirms discriminant validity.

4.5.6.2 Propensity Score Matching

To replicate the results of Studies 1 and 2 and to analyze in a field study whether rejection from a product test has negative and positive effects on purchase intention and the intention to spread negative WOM (H1/H2), the data from the pre- and post-treatment surveys are used. The differences and changes in the pre- and post-treatment survey data are examined. In order to assess the differences between participants regarding psychological mechanisms and behavioral changes before and after the product test, the focus is on those participants who took part in both the pre- and post-treatment surveys. This means that a total of 112 students are considered, of whom 84 did not apply and 28 did apply (Fig. 4.11: rejected applicants: N=23; accepted applicants: N=5). However, the five product testers are also excluded from further analysis, so that non-applicants are compared with rejected applicants. The individual participant codes are used to identify the differences between the data before and after the product test and to determine whether the participant applied for the product test and received a rejection.

Since participants were not randomly selected as product testers but instead joined the experimental group through self-initiated applications, rejected applicants may systematically differ from non-applicants in the control group. Statistical matching can mitigate the problem of self-selection (Rosenbaum/Rubin 1985, p. 35). It has already been widely applied in statistics (Rosenbaum/Rubin 1985), economics (Dehejia/Wahba 2002, Hirano/Imbens/Ridder 2003), and the marketing literature (Eggert/Steinhoff/Witte 2019; Huang et al. 2012). In this approach, a randomized experiment is simulated using covariates to create an artificial control group that closely resembles the experimental group (Rubin/Stuart 2006, p. 1,814 ff.). Once a well-matched control group has been established, differences between the treatment recipients and the control group can be analyzed by comparing the two groups (Wangenheim/Bayón 2007, p. 40). In this field study, propensity score matching is applied (Eggert/Steinhoff/Witte 2019, Harmeling et al.

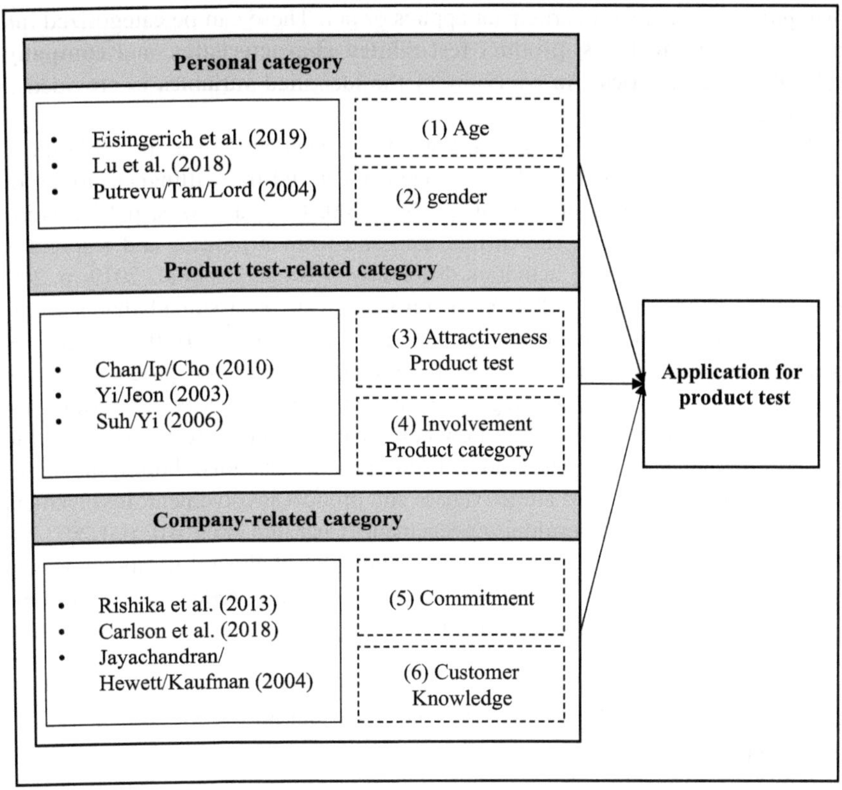

Fig. 4.12 Identified matching variables of the field study. (*Source:* Own representation)

2015, Kumar et al. 2016), which is particularly suitable for reducing the dimensionality problem when many covariates are present that could lead to self-selection effects, as it consolidates all covariates into a single scale—the probability of receiving the treatment (Stuart 2010, p. 8).

Propensity score matching consists of **four steps** (Garnefeld et al. 2013, p. 18; Wangenheim/Bayón 2007, p. 40). **The first step** is to identify predictors for the treatment (the application) as independent variables (Caliendo/Kopeinig 2008, p. 38). In this study, determinants are identified to model the participant's decision to apply for the product test. In total, six determinants were identified that may influence whether a participant applies or not. These can be categorized into **personal characteristics, product test-related characteristics**, and **company-related characteristics**. An overview of the identified variables is provided in Fig. 4.12.

In the **personal** category, age and gender were identified as possible determinants. Age has a positive effect on engagement and the willingness to act on behalf of a brand (Eisingerich et al. 2019, p. 200; Lu et al. 2018, p. 85). Moreover, several studies have shown that men and women process and respond to advertising and marketing activities differently (Eisingerich et al. 2019, p. 200; Putrevu/Tan/Lord 2004, p. 20 ff.). Therefore, it can be assumed that age and gender influence whether a person applies for a product test. In the category of **product test-related** characteristics, the attractiveness of the product test and involvement in the product category were identified as possible determinants. The decision to apply depends on how attractive the product test is perceived to be and how involved the applicant is in the product category. Future intentions are influenced by perceived attractiveness and product involvement. Involvement affects attitudes and the resulting engagement (Chan/Ip/Cho 2010, p. 1,207; Yi/Jeon 2003, p. 229; Suh/Yi 2006, p. 145). Thus, the likelihood of applying may depend on how attractive the person perceives the test product to be and how involved they are in the product category.

Table 4.7 Determinants of application: Pre- and post-treatment survey

Pre- and Post-Treatment Survey		
Exogenous Variable	Regression Coefficient	Wald
Constant	–5.63	3.82
Personal Category		
Age	0.06	0.38
Gender	–0.38	0.56
Product Test-Related Category		
Attractiveness of the Product Test	0.57*	5.72
Involvement with Product Category	–0.09	0.23
Company-Related Category		
Commitment	0.21	1.11
Customer Knowledge	0.14	0.78

*** $p < 0.001$; ** $p < 0.01$; * $p < 0.05$
Source: Own illustration.

In addition, commitment and customer knowledge were identified as **company-related** factors that influence the application decision. Commitment affects customers' future behavior and thus their participation in product tests (Rishika et al. 2013, p. 124 ff.). Some applicants hope to provide feedback to the company through the product test, in the form of customer knowledge, and thereby help the company (Carlson et al. 2018, p. 28; Jayachandran/Hewett/Kaufman 2004, p. 229 f.). Therefore, a person's application may depend on how emotionally connected they feel to the company and how highly they value their customer knowledge.

In the **second step**, the propensity score is calculated using a binary logistic regression. The score represents the probability of the event occurring (Eggert/Steinhoff/Witte 2019, p. 121), in this case, the likelihood that participants apply for the product test (Table 4.7). The results of the logistic regression confirm the effect of the attractiveness of the product test ($ß=0.57$, $SE=0.24$, $p=0.02$) on the application decision. In contrast, age ($ß=0.06$, $SE=0.10$, $p=0.54$), gender ($ß=-0.38$, $SE=0.51$, $p=0.46$), involvement with the product category ($ß=-0.09$, $SE=0.18$, $p=0.63$), commitment ($ß=0.21$, $SE=0.20$, $p=0.29$), and customer knowledge ($ß=0.14$, $SE=0.15$, $p=0.38$) did not have a significant influence as antecedent variables on the application. Nevertheless, all theoretically derived covariates were included in the matching model to calculate the propensity score (Rubin/Thomas 1996, p. 253).

In the **third step** of propensity score matching, each treatment case is matched with a non-treatment case. Nearest neighbor matching was used, in which the treatment case is paired with the non-treatment case whose propensity score is closest. To address the issue that some cases may not achieve a good match with this method and to define a tolerance range, the caliper matching method is applied. The tolerance range specifies the maximum difference between the probabilities of the two matched cases (Wangenheim/Bayón 2007, p. 40 f.). In this field study, treatment and non-treatment cases are matched using the caliper matching procedure. The treatment case is matched with its nearest neighbor if the two propensity scores fall within the specified tolerance range (Cochran/Rubin 1973, p. 420; Eggert/Steinhoff/Witte 2019, p. 121). The matching procedure links each rejected applicant with a statistical twin from the control group who did not apply for the product test but, statistically, had the same likelihood of doing so. Based on Silverman's rule (1986, p. 45), a maximum difference of 0.07 in the propensity scores of paired participants was determined. Even with this strict rule, a statistical twin was found for 23 out of 23 (100%) rejected applicants. The matched sample thus consists of 46 participants, half of whom were rejected and the other half did not apply for the product test.

In the **fourth step** of propensity score matching, the matching quality and the percentage reduction in bias (PRB) (Rosenbaum/Rubin 1985, p. 35) are assessed. Testing for significant differences in the means of the covariates between the experimental and control groups verifies that, prior to matching, the cases in both groups differ statistically in their observed characteristics and behavior. After matching, however, the means of the covariates in both groups are nearly identical, indicating a successful adjustment for self-selection. The average PRB for all significant predictors is 68%, suggesting a reduction in self-selection bias (Table 4.8).

4.5.6.3 Difference-in-Differences Estimation

The matched sample of participants is analyzed below using a difference-in-differences approach. Combining propensity score matching with a difference-in-differences estimation has proven to be less susceptible to bias than all other known methods for evaluating treatment effects (Eggert/Steinhof/Witte 2019; Heckman/Ichimura/Todd 1997; Wangenheim/Bayón 2007). In this study, the difference-in-differences approach is used to examine the behavior of participants in the experimental group (those who applied for the product test and were rejected) and the control group (those who did not apply for the product test) before and after the product test. The differences between rejected applicants and non-applicants are analyzed with respect to purchase intention (i.e., purchase intention after treatment minus purchase intention before treatment), intention to spread negative WOM, perceived skepticism, and commitment. This approach controls for both time-invariant participant characteristics and time trend effects, and helps to identify the causal effect of rejection on customer behavior (Bleier/Harmeling/Palmatier 2018; Eggert/Steinhoff/Witte 2019; Janakiraman/Lim/Rishika 2018).

4.5.6.4 Hypothesis Testing

To test Hypotheses 1 and 2, the PROCESS procedure (Hayes 2018) is applied using difference-in-differences estimators on the matched sample. Model 4 (5,000 samples) is first used to analyze whether the differences in perceived skepticism and commitment mediate the effect of a rejection on the differences in purchase intentions. The indirect effect via perceived skepticism ($b = -0.01$, $SE = 0.06$, 90% $CI = [-0.11, 0.10]$) on purchase intention is not significant. Thus, Hypothesis H1a is not supported in this study either. Since the price of the test product in the field study was comparatively low, this is consistent with the results from Study 1 and Study 2. Applicants only become skeptical if the test products are more expensive or if they are rejected more frequently. The indirect

Table 4.8 Means before and after matching

Before matching (means)			Variable	After matching (means)			PRB
Control group No application (n=84)	Experim. group Rejection (n=23)	***p***-value	Control group	Control group No application (n=23)	Experim. group Rejection (n=23)	***p***-value	
5.11	5.87	0.01*	Attractiveness of product test	5.62	5.87	0.56	67.60 %
							67.60 %

*** $p < 0.001$; ** $p < 0.01$; * $p < 0.05$
Experim. group = Experimental group
Source: Own illustration based on Garnefeld et al. 2013, p. 21.

effect via commitment ($b=0.26$, $SE=0.15$, 90% $CI=[0.03, 0.50]$) on purchase intention is significant, which supports H2a.

A closer look at the significant positive effect of rejection on perceived commitment reveals an increase of 0.78 on the 7-point Likert scale for commitment after the rejection. Figure 4.13 shows the means and changes in commitment for the experimental and control groups. After matching, prior to the product test, there is a non-significant difference of 0.10 in commitment. Thus, the two groups did not differ in their commitment levels before the product test was conducted. This again demonstrates the effectiveness of the matching. After the rejection, however, rejected applicants show a significantly higher average commitment than non-applicants: with a commitment level of 3.23, they have a commitment that is 0.78 higher than non-applicants, whose average commitment level is 2.45. This corresponds to a 32% increase in commitment.

The direct effect of a rejection on purchase intention in PROCESS Model 4 is not significant ($t=-1.41$, $p=0.16$, 90% $CI=[-0.99, 0.09]$). The total effect of a rejection (compared to no application) on purchase intention is also not significant ($b=-0.20$, $SE=0.32$, 90% $CI=[-0.75, 0.34]$).

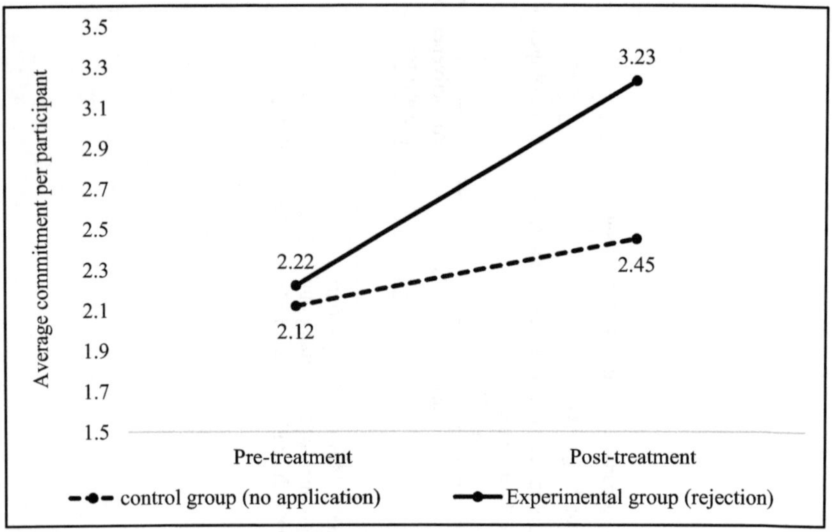

Fig. 4.13 Development of commitment among rejected applicants and non-applicants. (*Source:* Own illustration)

Subsequently, it is examined whether the differences in perceived skepticism and commitment mediate the effect of a rejection on the intention to spread negative WOM. Contrary to Hypotheses H1b and H2b, there is neither a significant indirect effect via perceived skepticism ($b = 0.02$, $SE = 1.11$, 90% CI = [−1.73, 1.74]) nor via commitment ($b = -1.71$, $SE = 2.31$, 90% CI = [−5.80, 1.64]) on the intention to spread negative WOM. The direct effect of a rejection in the product test on the intention to spread negative WOM is not significant ($t = 0.30$, $p = 0.76$, 90% CI = [−9.29, 0.08]). The total effect of a rejection (compared to non-application) on the intention to spread negative WOM is also not significant ($b = 0.35$, $SE = 6.31$, 90% CI = [−10.25, 10.95]).

4.5.6.5 Post-hoc Analysis

Up to this point, the focus has been on purchase intention and the intention to spread negative WOM as dependent variables. However, the data from the field study also allow for the tracking and analysis of actual engagement behavior as an additional dependent variable. Customers can create value for a company through their participation (e.g., taking part in surveys for feedback, co-creation, or development processes). Consequently, the extent to which customers are willing to engage can influence a company's value (Kumar et al. 2010, p. 307). In the field study, engagement was operationalized as participation in the post-treatment survey, and it was compared whether a rejection affects engagement, i.e., participation in the post-treatment survey.

The commitment-consistency principle can explain not only the relationship between a rejection and the purchase intention of the rejected applicant, but also the relationship between rejection and the engagement of the rejected applicant. According to Cialdini (2007, p. 43), there is a desire to be consistent with what one has already done (and to appear so). This social-psychological phenomenon can influence not only the resulting commitment, but also the future engagement of rejected applicants. If a company succeeds in convincing a person to apply for a product test, the person actively chooses this action. Thus, the person takes an active step by applying, which sets the mechanism of consistent behavior in motion. As a result, the applicant now feels both internal and external pressure to continue engaging with the company in the future.

This desire for engagement was already evident in the interviews of the first exploratory study with rejected applicants. It became clear that a rejection for the product test does not negatively affect the relationship with the company, since the person has once actively chosen to engage with the company. The rejected applicants were actually more motivated to apply again for a product test with the company and to continue participating in product tests:

"I felt motivated to apply for more to be successful in future." (*male, 30*)

"I ended up applying for more out of a desire to be more successful going forward." (*male, 33*)

"I do not let something like this to put me off applying for future opportunities for product testing." (*female, 79*)

"I had another chance to try again the next time, they had a product to test." (*female, 27*)

"I was motivated to apply for the next hoping I would be a good fit." (*female, 24*)

To analyze whether a rejection in a product testing program has a positive effect on the engagement of rejected applicants, data from the pre-treatment survey are used and participation in the post-treatment survey is analyzed. For this reason, the sample used changes for the post-hoc analysis. Figure 4.14 shows the distribution of participants across the groups.

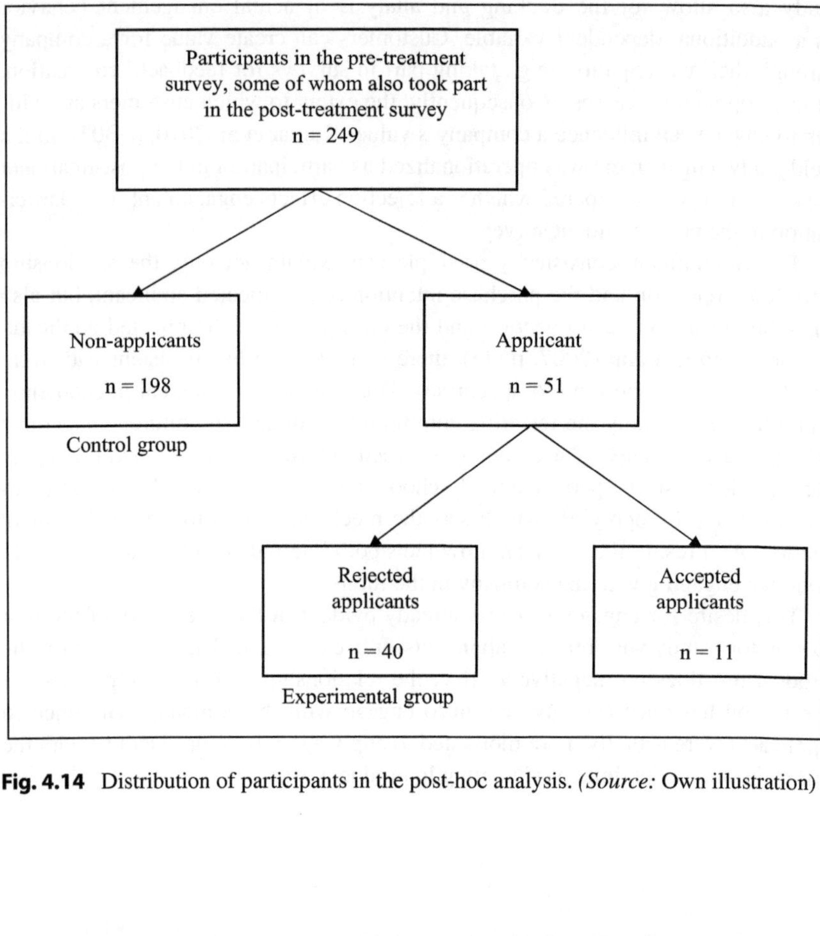

Fig. 4.14 Distribution of participants in the post-hoc analysis. (*Source:* Own illustration)

Within this sample of 249 students, all of whom participated in at least the pre-treatment survey and some also in the post-treatment survey, 51 students applied for the product test and 198 did not. Of these 51 applicants, 40 were rejected and 11 were selected as product testers. In the analysis, the rejected applicants are compared with those who did not apply (control group).

Participant engagement after the product test is measured by participation in the post-treatment survey. Using the individual codes of the participants, it can be determined which participants also took part in the post-treatment survey and whether they applied and received a rejection. As in the hypothesis testing, propensity score matching and logistic regression are used as analytical methods.

As in hypothesis testing, **propensity score matching** is also used in the post-hoc test to address the problem of self-selection. Analogous to the previous analysis, propensity score matching is conducted following the **four-step procedure**. The **first step** involves identifying the predictors for treatment as independent variables. Previously, determinants explaining the application decision were identified in order to model the participant's decision to apply for the product test (Caliendo/Kopeinig 2008, p. 38). In total, six variables from the pre-treatment survey were identified as responsible for whether a participant applies or not. These can be categorized into personal, product test-related, and company-related characteristics. The same identified determinants are also used in the post-hoc analysis, as some participants are the same and the probability of applying to be calculated remains unchanged.

In the **second step**, the propensity score is calculated using a binary logistic regression. Here, too, the probability of applying for the product test is calculated for each participant (Table 4.9). The binary logistic regression includes all participants who took part in the pre-treatment survey. The results of the logistic regression confirm the effects of product test attractiveness ($ß=0.61$, $SE=0.18$, $p<0.001$), involvement with the product category ($ß=-0.27$, $SE=0.13$, $p=0.04$), and commitment ($ß=0.32$, $SE=0.14$, $p=0.02$) on the application decision. However, age ($ß=-0.04$, $SE=0.07$, $p=0.54$), gender ($ß=-0.18$, $SE=0.38$, $p=0.63$), and customer knowledge ($ß=0.13$, $SE=0.12$, $p=0.26$) did not have a significant effect. Nevertheless, all theoretically derived covariates are included in the matching model to calculate the propensity score.

In the **third step** of propensity score matching, each treatment case is matched with a non-treatment case. Here, the caliper matching method is again used for the assignment. Based on Silverman's rule (1986, p. 45), a maximum difference of 0.04 in the propensity scores of paired participants is set. Even with this strict rule, statistical twins can be assigned for 39 out of 40 (97.5%) rejected applicants,

Table 4.9 Determinants of application pre-treatment survey

Pre-Treatment Survey		
Exogenous Variable	Regression Coefficient	Wald
Constant	−3.59	3.65
Personal Category		
Age	−0.04	0.37
Gender	−0.18	0.24
Product Test-Related Category		
Product Test Attractiveness	0.61***	11.47
Product Category Involvement	−0.27*	4.173
Company-Related Category		
Commitment	0.32*	5.27
Customer Knowledge	0.13	1.25

*** $p < 0.001$; ** $p < 0.01$; * $p < 0.05$
Source: Own illustration.

which represents a good rate. The matched sample thus consists of 78 participants, half of whom were rejected and half of whom did not apply for the product test.

In the **fourth step** of propensity score matching, the matching quality and the percentage reduction in bias (PRB) are assessed. The matching quality and PRB for the matches are recalculated. Testing for significant differences in the means of the covariates between the experimental and control groups shows that customers in both groups were statistically different in the original sample. After the matching procedure, the means of both groups are nearly identical; this implies a successful adjustment for self-selection. The average PRB for all significant predictors is 82%, indicating a strong overall reduction in bias due to self-selection (Table 4.10).

To test whether a rejection has a positive effect on participant engagement, a logistic regression is conducted with the matched sample. The results of the logistic regression show that significantly more participants took part in the post-treatment survey if they had received a rejection than if they had not applied (ß = 2.18, SE = 0.48, $p < 0.001$). Thus, rejection in the product test has a positive impact on the engagement of rejected applicants.

Table 4.10 Means before and after matching: Post-hoc analysis

Before matching (means)			Variable	After matching (means)			PRB
Control group: No application (n = 198)	Experimental group: Rejection (n = 40)	*p*-value		Control group: No application (n = 39)	Experimental group: Rejection (n = 39)	*p*-value	
4.97	5.75	0.001**	Product test attractiveness	5.63	5.75	0.67	84.70%
1.86	2.43	0.009**	Commitment	2.50	2.38	0.72	78.90%
							81.80%

*** $p < 0.001$; ** $p < 0.01$; * $p < 0.05$
Source: Own illustration based on Garnefeld et al., 2013, p. 21.

Table 4.10 Means before and after matching for post hoc analysis

Variable	Before matching (means)			After matching (means)			%RB
	Control group: No application group (n = [illegible])	Experimental group: Rejection group	p-value	Control group: No application group (n = [illegible])	Experimental group: Rejection (n = [illegible])	p-value	
Product test attractiveness	4.97	5.58	0.015*	5.02	5.58	0.07	84.20%
Commitment	1.60	1.45	0.009**	[illegible]	[illegible]	0.79	78.90%
							81.20%

*** p ≤ 0.001, ** p ≤ 0.01, * p ≤ 0.05

Source: Own illustration based on Garnefeld et al. 2019a, p. [illegible]

Conclusion 5

Chapter 5 provides the concluding discussion of this work. In this chapter, the research questions formulated in the first chapter are answered, implications for marketing research and practice are outlined, and the limitations of the study are discussed. The chapter begins with a summary of the findings (**Sect. 5.1**). This is followed by a discussion of the implications for marketing research and practice (**Sect. 5.2**), before concluding with a consideration of the study's limitations and an outlook on future research needs (**Sect. 5.3**).

5.1 Summary of Findings

Within the framework of online product testing programs, many applicants receive a rejection from the company and thus do not receive a test product. The starting point of this study was the assumption that rejections in online product testing programs can lead to both negative and positive consequences for the rejecting company. The scientific investigation therefore aimed to answer the overarching research question: How does a rejection in an online product testing program affect the rejected applicant? In addition, the following three sub-questions were addressed:

1. Which psychological mechanisms explain the effects of a rejection in an online product testing program? Are there both positive and negative mechanisms at work?
2. Under what conditions does the effect of a rejection in an online product testing program occur?
3. How does a rejection influence the future behavior of rejected applicants?

K. L. Küpper, *Negative and Positive Effects of Rejections in Online Product Testing Programs*, https://doi.org/10.1007/978-3-658-49277-9_5

The conceptual foundations made it clear that online product testing programs, as a marketing tool, share similarities with product sampling but also exhibit important differences, such as implementation, the completeness of the product, and obligations following application. The literature review revealed an initial research gap, as there is currently little research on online product testing programs. In examining rejections, it also became apparent that, while there is extensive research in social psychology and human resource management on the effects and influencing factors of rejections, rejections in a marketing context have received little attention to date. Only stockouts, as a form of rejection in marketing, have been studied in more detail. However, these differ significantly from rejections in online product testing programs, revealing another research gap: there is no research on the effects of and factors influencing rejections in online product testing programs.

To answer the research questions, a total of 12 hypotheses were derived based on an exploratory qualitative survey and the theoretical foundations. These were subsequently tested in two scenario experiments and a field study that combined propensity score matching with a difference-in-differences estimation.

Overall, the results of **Study 1** show that rejections in online product testing programs can lead to both negative and positive consequences for the rejecting company. A rejection increases the perceived commitment of rejected applicants, which in turn leads to a higher purchase intention among these applicants (Hypothesis H2a). However, if the price of the test product is high, a rejection increases the perceived skepticism of rejected applicants. This leads to a decrease in purchase intention and an increase in the intention to spread negative word-of-mouth (Hypotheses H3a and H3c). The remaining hypotheses could not be confirmed or were not tested in this study.

The results from **Study 2** again confirmed the positive consequences for the rejecting company. In this study as well, a rejection increased the perceived commitment of rejected applicants, which in turn led to a higher purchase intention (Hypothesis H2a). In this scenario experiment, the number of previous rejections was examined as a contextual factor, and it was found that repeated rejections can have negative consequences for companies. Multiple rejections increase the perceived skepticism of rejected applicants. This leads to a decrease in purchase intention and an increase in the intention to spread negative word-of-mouth (Hypotheses H4a and H4c). The remaining hypotheses could not be confirmed or were not tested in this study.

Study 3 then focused on testing the hypotheses in the field without moderation or contextual variables. Consistent with Studies 1 and 2, the field study also found that the perceived commitment of rejected applicants increased after a rejection. This led to a higher purchase intention (Hypothesis H2a). The remaining hypotheses could not be confirmed or were not tested in this study. In addition, another positive effect for companies was observed in the field. After a rejection, the engagement of rejected applicants increased. Significantly more rejected applicants participated in the post-treatment survey than non-applicants.

In summary, this means that a rejection can lead to both negative and positive consequences for the rejecting company. This study identifies psychological mechanisms that explain the effects of a rejection (**Research Question 1**). A rejection can trigger skepticism in the rejected applicant. This arises through the attribution process initiated to understand the possible reasons for the rejection. However, the emergence of skepticism depends on contextual factors and does not always occur. At the same time, the rejected applicant may experience a sense of commitment after the rejection. This commitment is based on the active decision to apply and increases after a rejection in an online product testing program.

Furthermore, this study examined two different contextual conditions. It was shown under which conditions the effect of a rejection in an online product testing program occurs (**Research Question 2**). A rejection in an online product testing program only increases the perceived skepticism of rejected applicants if the company offers high-priced test products. For high-priced test products, companies must expect negative consequences due to the increase in perceived skepticism. The price of the test product has no significant effect on the impact of a rejection on perceived commitment and subsequent behavior of rejected applicants. Another contextual factor influencing the perceived skepticism of rejected applicants is the number of previous rejections. If a company rejects an applicant multiple times (three or ten times), perceived skepticism increases. Applicants rejected for the third time are significantly more skeptical than those rejected for the first time. Applicants who have been rejected as product testers by the company for the tenth time are even more skeptical. The number of previous rejections has no significant effect on perceived commitment.

The question of how a rejection influences the future behavior of rejected applicants can also be answered (**Research Question 3**). If a rejected applicant feels skepticism due to a high product price or multiple previous rejections, their purchase intention decreases. At the same time, the intention to spread negative word-of-mouth about the company increases. The commitment that arises leads to an increase in purchase intention among rejected applicants.

5.2 Implications for Marketing Research and Practice

This section outlines the relevant findings for marketing research and practice. The following presents the implications for marketing research first (**Sect. 5.2.1**), followed by the implications for marketing practice (**Sect. 5.2.2**).

5.2.1 Implications for Marketing Research

This study has **three implications** for marketing research. **First**, the negative and positive effects of rejections on unsuccessful applicants in online product testing programs highlight the need for further theoretical and empirical work focused on understanding the impact of rejections. The current state of research on rejections in marketing is still very limited. Additional studies are needed to expand this body of knowledge and to understand the inconsistent findings in product sampling research. Fombelle and colleagues (2016, p. 685) found negative effects of rejections in marketing on the continued participation of rejected applicants, but Piezunka and Dahlander (2019, p. 521) point out that rejections can also be interpreted as feedback and may be appreciated by rejected participants (Fombelle/Bone/Lemon 2016, p. 685; Piezunka/Dahlander 2019, p. 521).

Rejections differ across various disciplines (social psychology, human resource management, and marketing). A rejection in a product testing program is characterized by the fact that it is issued by the company, the rejected applicant often does not know the reasons for the rejection, and may feel personally rejected as an individual, since they had to apply personally and in writing. Previous research on rejections in interpersonal relationships or human resource management, on stock-outs, rejections in co-creation contexts, or in the context of losing a competition or sweepstakes, cannot adequately address the specific effects of rejections in product testing programs. This study thus provides initial insights to help close these research gaps: it demonstrates positive effects of rejections in online product testing programs. The increase in purchase intention and engagement among rejected applicants is a behavior desired by companies. In addition, several context-specific factors have been identified that can lead to negative effects.

Second, this study underscores the importance of considering various, potentially contradictory theoretical mechanisms when anticipating the outcomes of online product testing programs. The results suggest that multiple psychological mechanisms coexist in customers' minds, as shown in other research studies (Steinhoff/Palmatier 2016; Eggert/Steinhoff/Garnefeld 2015). Theoretically, two opposing mechanisms are derived and experimentally confirmed that explain the effects of product testing programs on purchase intentions and intentions to spread negative WOM: perceived skepticism and perceived commitment. On the one hand, rejected applicants want to know the reasons for their rejection. Since rejected applicants seek to protect themselves or may not be aware of all the background processes of the product test, it is easy for the attribution process to fail, leading them to question the company's true motives behind the product test. As a result, rejected applicants become skeptical and are likely less inclined to purchase the test product after being rejected. At the same time, they may be more likely to spread negative WOM. On the other hand, people strive to behave consistently and are accordingly pressured by society. Once a person has actively decided in favor of something, they rarely change their mind or direction. This suggests that rejected individuals may still want to test and subsequently purchase the product after being rejected.

Third, this study emphasizes the importance of paying attention to contextual factors, as price and the number of previous rejections influence the mediating role of skepticism. A rejection in an online product testing program leads to an increase in perceived skepticism for high-priced test products. Similarly, skepticism increases when the applicant has already been rejected multiple times. Studies that neglect contextual factors may therefore lead to misleading conclusions.

5.2.2 Implications for Marketing Practice

The insights gained regarding the effects of rejections in online product testing programs allow for relevant recommendations for marketing practice. Key implications arise for the implementation of online product testing programs, particularly concerning awareness of potential negative and positive effects of rejections and the design of such programs.

In marketing practice, managers can benefit from the findings of this study in several ways. **First**, the study demonstrates that it is important for companies not to focus solely on accepted applicants, but also to consider rejected applicants in order to anticipate potential negative and positive effects of rejections. While a rejection increases the perceived commitment of the rejected applicant toward the company, under certain conditions it can also increase the perceived skepticism of rejected applicants. If a company ignores the negative effects of rejection and focuses only on the positive effects for accepted applicants, the evaluation of the program's effectiveness will be flawed. The findings of this study highlight the importance of rejection management. Companies should therefore carefully calculate the return on marketing of a product test (Reinecke/Tomczak 2006, p. 5 ff.; Rust/Lemon/Zeithaml 2004, p. 109 f.). They must consider not only the positive effects on accepted applicants, but also the negative and positive effects on rejected applicants. In this way, they can determine the optimal number of participants for their programs to increase profitability. If companies wish to reduce or avoid negative effects due to harmful WOM behavior, they should consider accepting more or all applicants, if possible. This would allow companies to benefit from the positive effects of rejected applicants while mitigating the negative impacts.

Second, the identification of negative effects of rejection in an online product testing program calls for caution among managers. However, this study also shows under which contextual conditions rejected applicants experience skepticism. Thus, managers can manage negative effects through targeted program design.

Third, managers should pay attention to the price of the test product when designing the program. The results suggest that rejection particularly triggers skepticism when the applicant suspects hidden motives behind the product test due to the company's high investment or repeated rejections. Managers should therefore consider the price of the test product in order to maintain the positive effects of commitment and reduce the negative effects of skepticism. If the company selects a high-priced test product, rejected applicants may respond with greater skepticism. Therefore, managers should, where possible, choose low-priced test products to avoid skepticism following a rejection. If a company offers high-priced test products, managers should try to reduce skepticism in order to increase purchase intention and prevent negative WOM. There are three ways to reduce the skepticism of rejected applicants: First, the selection process for product testers should be made as transparent as possible so that rejected applicants can understand the reasons for their rejection. In addition, companies can provide further information about the product test, such as the number of available test products, to counter the suspicion that there are no test products at all. Finally, companies can also publish the results and feedback from previous product testers to demonstrate that the advertised test products are indeed distributed.

Fourth, managers should also consider applicants' previous rejections. When an applicant is rejected by the company for the first time, the company benefits from their increased commitment. The manager's goal should then be to further increase this commitment in order to maximize purchase intention. One possible course of action is to make the application process attractive, making the test product more appealing and a repeat application more likely. However, from the third rejection onward, the skepticism of rejected applicants increases. Managers should seek to prevent this. Here too, those responsible should make the selection process for product testers as transparent as possible so that rejected applicants can understand the reasons for their rejection and may be less skeptical after multiple rejections. Furthermore, companies can ensure that applicants are selected as testers on their next application by tracking the number of applications. In this way, they can prevent applicants from being rejected multiple times and can immediately inform rejected applicants that they will be given preference in the next product test if they reapply, in order to reduce skepticism.

5.3 Limitations and Directions for Future Research

The present study represents the first investigation of the relationship between rejections and purchase intention as well as the intention to spread negative word-of-mouth. The limitations of this work point to opportunities for future research. **First**, the study focuses on rejections in online product testing programs. As outlined in the conceptual foundations, rejections have primarily been studied in social psychology (Leary 2001; Williams/Zadro 2001) and human resource management (Gilliland 1993; Horvath/Ryan/Stierwart 2000), but have received little attention in marketing to date. The most frequently occurring phenomenon, stockouts, provides the majority of insights regarding the effects of a rejection and the factors influencing its perception (Ge/Messinger/Li 2009; Wangenheim/Bayón 2007; Helm/Hegenbart/Endres 2013). In contrast, the rejection of consumer ideas and the loss of a competition or game have so far only been considered to a limited extent. Future studies should seek to further close the research gap on rejections in marketing and expand the currently limited findings on rejections, for example in the co-creation context (Fombelle/Bone/Lemon 2016). Furthermore, in product testing programs, full-fledged products are distributed to testers. For future research, it may also be of interest to examine rejections for a service, as it is conceivable that product tests involving services could be offered in the future. It remains to be determined whether service companies would also be likely to experience negative and positive effects if they conducted a product test and rejected applicants.

Second, further studies can build on the findings of the present work and test other context-specific factors. The consideration of contextual factors is of great importance in marketing research (Garnefeld/Helm/Eggert 2011, p. 101). Some product testing programs, for example, require applicants to complete only a short questionnaire, while others expect a detailed letter of motivation. Thus, the effort invested by the applicant in the application process may influence the effects of rejection. According to Rafaeli (1999, p. 710), the time invested is a predictor of an applicant's reaction in the job application process. In the field study, students only had to complete a short questionnaire for their application, so this contextual factor could also be examined in future research. In addition, the wording of the rejection letter may also play a role. Gilliland et al. (2001, p. 669) have already found in their studies that the wording of the rejection influences the feelings of rejected applicants. If the company conveys a sense of fairness through the phrasing of the rejection, rejected applicants perceive the rejection in the selection process as less negative. In the co-creation context as well, it has been shown that formulating the rejection as friendly feedback can increase loyalty to the company (Piezunka/Dahlander 2019, p. 521).

Third, the dependent variables examined in the present study (purchase intention and intention to spread negative word-of-mouth) are operationalized as behavioral intentions. Only in the post-hoc analysis is the engagement of rejected applicants measured as actual behavior. In marketing research, behavioral intention is used as a good indicator of actual behavior (Ajzen 1985, p. 18; Ajzen 1991, pp. 181 f.; Fishbein/Ajzen 1975, pp. 368 f.), but future research should also measure actual purchase behavior and negative word-of-mouth behavior to further enhance external validity.

References

Aaker, David A.; Kumar, V.; Leone, Robert P.; Day, George S. (2013): Marketing research. International student version. 11th edn. Singapore: Wiley.

Adams, J. Stacy (1965): Inequity in social exchange. In: Advances in experimental social psychology, Bd. 2: Elsevier, pp. 267–299.

Adler, Alfred (1930): The education of children. London: George Allen & Unwin Ltd.

Ainsworth, Mary D. S. (1989): Attachments beyond infancy. In: *American Psychologist* 44 (4), pp. 709–716.

Ajzen, Icek (1985): From intentions to actions: A theory of planned behavior. In: Julius Kuhl and Jürgen Beckmann (eds.): Action control. From cognition to behavior. Berlin Heidelberg: Springer, pp. 11–39.

Ajzen, Icek (1991): The theory of planned behavior. In: *Organizational Behavior and Human Decision Processes* 50 (2), pp. 179–211.

Aral, Sinan; Muchnik, Lev; Sundararajan, Arun (2013): Engineering social contagions: Optimal network seeding in the presence of homophily. In: *Network Science* 1 (2), pp. 125–153.

Ambrose, Maureen L.; Cropanzano, Russell (2003): A longitudinal analysis of organizational fairness: An examination of reactions to tenure and promotion decisions. In: *Journal of Applied Psychology* 88 (2), pp. 266–275.

Baca-Motes, Katie; Brown, Amber; Gneezy, Ayelet; Keenan, Elizabeth A.; Nelson, Leif D. (2013): Commitment and Behavior Change: Evidence from the Field. In: *Journal of Consumer Research* 39 (5), pp. 1070–1084.

Bauer, Talya N.; Maertz, Jr., Carl P.; Dolen, Michael R.; Campion, Michael A. (1998): Longitudinal assessment of applicant reactions to employment testing and test outcome feedback. In: *Journal of Applied Psychology* 83 (6), pp. 892–903.

Baum, Daniela; Spann, Martin; Füller, Johann; Thürridl, Carina (2019): The impact of social media campaigns on the success of new product introductions. In: *Journal of Retailing and Consumer Services* 50, pp. 289–297.

Baumeister, Roy F.; Leary, Mark R. (1995): The need to belong: Desire for interpersonal attachments as a fundamental human motivation. In: *Psychological Bulletin* 117 (3), pp. 497–529.

K. Küpper, *Negative and Positive Effects of Rejections in Online Product Testing Programs*, https://doi.org/10.1007/978-3-658-49277-9

Bawa, Kapil; Shoemaker, Robert (2004): The effects of free sample promotions on incremental brand sales. In: *Marketing Science* 23 (3), pp. 345–363.

Bergkvist, Lars; Rossiter, John R. (2007): The Predictive Validity of Multiple-Item versus Single-Item Measures of the Same Constructs. In: *Journal of Marketing Research* 44(2), pp. 175–184.

Bettinger, Charles O.; Dawson Jr., Lyndon E.; Wales, Hugh G. (1979): The impact of free-sample advertising. In: *Journal of Advertising Research* 19 (3), pp. 35–39.

Bleier, Alexander; Harmeling, Colleen M.; Palmatier, Robert W. (2018): Creating effective online customer experiences. In: Journal of Marketing 83 (2), pp. 1–22.

Bond, Samuel D.; He, Stephen X.; Wen, Wen (2019): Speaking for "free": Word of mouth in free-and paid-product settings. In: *Journal of Marketing Research* 56 (2), pp. 276–290.

Boyes, Mark E.; French, Davina J. (2009): Having a cyberball: Using a ball-throwing game as an experimental social stressor to examine the relationship between neuroticism and coping. In: *Personality and Individual Differences* 47 (5), pp. 396–401.

Burger, Jerry M. (1992): Desire for control. Personality, social, and clinical perspectives. 1st edn. New York: Springer Science & Business Media.

Caliendo, Marco; Kopeinig, Sabine (2008): Some practical guidance for the implementation of propensity score matching. In: *Journal of Economic Surveys* 22 (1), pp. 31–72.

Campbell, Donald T.; Stanley, Julian C. (1963): Experimental and quasi-experimental designs for research. Chicago: Rand McNally & Company.

Carlson, Jamie; Rahman, Mohammad; Voola, Ranjit; De Vries, Natalie (2018): Customer engagement behaviours in social media: Capturing innovation opportunities. In: *Journal of Services Marketing* 32 (1).

Chae, Inyoung; Stephen, Andrew T.; Bart, Yakov; Yao, Dai (2017): Spillover effects in seeded word-of-mouth marketing campaigns. In: *Marketing Science* 36 (1), pp. 89–104.

Chan, S. L.; Ip, W. H.; Cho, V. (2010): A model for predicting customer value from perspectives of product attractiveness and marketing strategy. In: *Expert Systems with Applications* 37 (2), pp. 1207–1215.

Chandukala, Sandeep R.; Dotson, Jeffrey P.; Liu, Qing (2017): An assessment of when, where and under what conditions in-store sampling is most effective. In: *Journal of Retailing* 93 (4), pp. 493–506.

Chellappa, Ramnath K.; Shivendu, Shivendu (2005): Managing piracy: Pricing and sampling strategies for digital experience goods in vertically segmented markets. In: Information Systems Research 16 (4), pp. 400–417.

Chen, Hong; Duan, Wenjing; Zhou, Wenqi (2017): The interplay between free sampling and word of mouth in the online software market. In: *Decision Support Systems* 95, pp. 82–90.

Cheng, Hsing Kenneth; Liu, Yipeng (2012): Optimal software free trial strategy: The impact of network externalities and consumer uncertainty. In: *Information Systems Research* 23 (2), pp. 488–504.

Cialdini, Robert B. (2007): Influence. The psychology of persuasion. 4th edn. New York: HarperCollins.

Cochran, William G.; Rubin; Donald B. (1973): Controlling bias in observational studies: A review. In: *Sankhyā: The Indian Journal of Statistics: Series A*, pp. 417–446.

Cronbach, Lee J. (1951): Coefficient alpha and the internal structure of tests. In: *Psychometrika* 16 (3), pp. 297–334.

Cui, Fang; Hu, Hai-hua; Cui, Wen-tian; Xie, Ying (2018): Seeding strategies for new product launch: The role of negative word-of-mouth. In: *PloS ONE* 13 (11), pp. 1–23.

Dehejia, Rajeev H.; Wahba, Sadek (2002): Propensity score-matching methods for nonexperimental causal studies. In: *The Review of Economics and Statistics* 84 (1), pp. 151–161.

Dm-drogerie markt (2023: Produkttester-Community von dm, online verfügbar unter: https://produkttester.dm.de/so-gehts, Accessed 04.09.2023.

Döring, Nicola (2023): Forschungsmethoden und Evaluation in den Sozial- und Humanwissenschaften, 6th edn., Berlin: Springer.

Döring, Nicola; Bortz, Jürgen (2016): Forschungsmethoden und Evaluation in den Sozial- und Humanwissenschaften. 5th edn. Berlin Heidelberg: Springer.

Dost, Florian; Phieler, Ulrike; Haenlein, Michael; Libai, Barak (2019): Seeding as part of the marketing mix: word-of-mouth program interactions for fast-moving consumer goods. In: *Journal of Marketing* 83 (2), pp. 62–81.

Dunn, Jennifer; Schweitzer, Maurice (2005): Feeling and Believing: The Influence of Emotion on Trust. In: *Journal of personality and social psychology* 88, pp. 736–748.

Eggert, Andreas; Steinhoff, Lena; Garnefeld, Ina (2015): Managing the bright and dark sides of status endowment in hierarchical loyalty programs. In: *Journal of Service Research* 18 (2), pp. 210–228.

Eggert, Andreas; Steinhoff, Lena; Witte, Carina (2019): Gift purchases as catalysts for strengthening customer–brand relationships. In: *Journal of Marketing* 83(5), pp. 115–132.

Eid, Michael; Gollwitzer, Mario; Schmitt, Manfred (2017): Statistik und Forschungsmethoden, 5th edn., Basel: Beltz Verlag.

Eifler, Stefanie; Leitgöb, Heinz (2019): Experiment. In: Baur, N., Blasius, J. (eds) Handbuch Methoden der empirischen Sozialforschung. Wiesbaden: Springer VS, pp. 225–241.

Eisingerich, Andreas B.; Marchand, André; Fritze, Martin P.; Dong, Lin (2019): Hook vs. hope: How to enhance customer engagement through gamification. In: *International Journal of Research in Marketing* 36 (2). pp. 200–215.

Eisenberger, Naomi I.; Lieberman, Matthew D.; Williams, Kipling D. (2003): Does rejection hurt? An fMRI study of social exclusion. In: *SCIENCE* 302, pp. 290–292.

Eroglu, S. (1987): The scenario method: A theoretical, not theatrical, approach. In: *1987 AMA Summer Marketing Educators' Conference Proceedings*, Chicago, p. 236.

Feinberg, Richard A.; Meoli-Stanton, Jennifer; Gable, Myron (1996): Employment rejection and acceptance letters and their unintended consequences on image, self-concept, and intentions. In: *Journal of Business and Psychology* 11 (1), pp. 63–71.

Festinger, Leon (1957): A theory of cognitive dissonance. Redwood City: Stanford University Press.

Fishbein, M.; Ajzen, Icek (1975): Belief, attitude, intention, and behavior: An introduction to theory and research. Reading, Ma: Addison-Wesley.

Fitzsimons, Gavan J. (2000): Consumer response to stockouts. In: *Journal of Consumer Research* 27 (2), pp. 249–266.

Fombelle, Paul W.; Bone, Sterling A.; Lemon, Katherine N. (2016): Responding to the 98%: Face-enhancing strategies for dealing with rejected customer ideas. In: *Journal of the Academy of Marketing Science* 44, pp. 685–706.

Forehand, M. R., & Grier, S. (2003): When is honesty the best policy? The effect of stated company intent on consumer skepticism. In: *Journal of Consumer Psychology, 13*(3), pp. 349–356.

Fornell, Claes; Larcker, David F. (1981): Evaluating structural equation models with unobservable variables and measurement error. In: *Journal of Marketing Research* 18 (1), pp. 39–50.

Foscht, T.; Angerer, T.: Swoboda, B. (2009): Mixed Methods. In: Buber, R., Holzmüller, Hartmut .H (eds.): Qualitative Marktforschung. Wiesbaden: Gabler, pp. 247–259.

Foubert, Bram; Gijsbrechts, Els (2016): Try it, you'll like it – or will you? The perils of early free-trial promotions for high-tech service adoption. In: *Marketing Science* 35 (5), pp. 810–826.

Freedman, Jonathan L.; Fraser, Scott C. (1966): Compliance without pressure: The foot-in-the-door technique. *Journal ol Personality and Social Psychology* 4 (2), pp. 195–202.

Fullerton, Gordon (2005): How commitment both enables and undermines marketing relationships. In: *European Journal of Marketing* 39 (11/12), pp. 1 372–1 388.

Garnefeld, Ina; Eggert, Andreas; Helm, Sabrina V.; Tax, Stephen S. (2013): Growing existing customers' revenue streams through customer referral programs. In: *Journal of Marketing* 77 (4), pp. 17–32.

Garnefeld, Ina; Helm, Sabrina; Eggert, Andreas (2011): Walk your talk: An experimental investigation of the relationship between word of mouth ad communicators' loyalty. In: *Journal of Service Research* 14 (1), pp. 93–107.

Garnefeld, Ina; Krah, Tabea; Böhm, Eva; Gremler, Dwayne D. (2021): Online reviews generated through product testing: Can more favorable reviews be enticed with free products? In: *Journal of the Academy of Marketing Science* 49 (4), pp. 703–722.

Garms-Homolová, Vjenka (2021): Sozialpsychologie der Informationsverarbeitung über das Selbst und die Mitmenschen – Selbstkonzept, Attributionstheorien, Stereotype & Vorurteile, Berlin: Springer.

Ge, Xin; Messinger, Paul R.; Li, Jin (2009): Influence of soldout products on consumer choice. In: *Journal of Retailing* 85 (3), pp. 274–287.

Gedenk, Karen (2009): Verkaufsförderung. In: Manfred Bruhn, Franz-Rudolf Esch and Tobias Langner (eds.): Handbuch Kommunikation. Grundlagen – Innovative Ansätze – Praktische Umsetzungen. Wiesbaden: Gabler, pp. 267–283.

Gedenk, Karen (1999): Die Wirkungen von Warenproben. In: *Zeitschrift für Betriebswirtschaft* (2/99), pp. 89–110.

Gedenk, Karen; Neslin, Scott A. (1999): The role of retail promotion in determining future brand loyalty: Its effect on purchase event feedback. In: *Journal of Retailing* 75 (4), pp. 433–459.

Gilliland, Stephen W. (1993): The perceived fairness of selection systems: An organizational justice perspective. In: *Academy of Management Review* 18 (4), pp. 694–734.

Gilliland, Stephen W.; Groth, Markus; Baker IV, Robert C; Dew, Angela F.; Polly, Lisa M.; Langdon, Jay C. (2001): Improving applicants' reactions to rejection letters: An application of fairness theory. In: *Personnel Psychology* 54 (3), pp. 669–703.

Gläser, Jochen; Laudel, Grit (2010): Experteninterviews und qualitative Inhaltsanalyse als Instrumente rekonstruierender Untersuchungen. 4th edn. Wiesbaden: VS Verlag.

Gnambs, Timo; Batinic, Bernad (2011): Qualitative Online-Forschung. In: Gabriele Naderer and Eva Balzer (eds.): Qualitative Marktforschung in Theorie und Praxis. Grundlagen – Methoden – Anwendungen. 2nd edn. Wiesbaden: Gabler Springer, pp. 385–404.

Gonzaga, Gian C.; Keltner, Dacher; Londahl, Esme A.; Smith, Michael D. (2001): Love and the commitment problem in romantic relations and friendship. In: *Journal of Personality and Social Psychology* 81 (2), pp. 247–262.

Gopinath, Mahesh; Nyer, Prashanth U. (2009): The effect of public commitment on resistance to persuasion: The influence of attitude certainty, issue importance, susceptibility to normative influence, preference for consistency and source proximity. In: *International Journal of Research in Marketing* 26(1), pp. 60–68

Groeger, Lars; Buttle, Francis (2014): Word-of-mouth marketing: Towards an improved understanding of multi-generational campaign reach. In: *European Journal of Marketing* 48 (7/8), pp. 1186–1208.

Haenlein, Michael; Libai, Barak (2013): Targeting revenue leaders for a new product. In: *Journal of Marketing* 77 (3), pp. 65–80.

Haenlein, Michael; Libai, Barak (2017): Seeding, referral, and recommendation: Creating profitable word-of-mouth programs. In: *California Management Review* 59 (2), pp. 68–91.

Hamilton, Rebecca; Thompson, Debora; Bone, Sterlin; Chaplin, Lan Nguyen; Griskevicus, Vladas; Goldsmith, Kelly; Hill, Ronald; John, Deborah Roedder; Mittal, Chiraag; O'Guinn, Tomas; Piff, Paul; Roux, Caroline; Shah, Anuj; Zhu, Meng (2019): The effects of scarcity on consumer decision journeys. In: *Jounral of the Academy of Marketing Science* 47, pp. 532–550.

Han, Yanqing; Zhang, Zongming (2018): Impact of free sampling on product diffusion based on Bass model. In: *Electronic Commerce Research* 18 (1), pp. 125–141.

Harmeling, Colleen M.; Palmatier, Robert W.; Houston, Mark B.; Arnold, Mark J.; Samaha, Stephen A. (2015): Transformational relationship events. In: *Journal of Marketing* 79 (5), pp. 39–62.

Hausknecht, John P.; Day, David V.; Thomas, Scott C. (2004): Applicant reactions to selection procedures: An updated model and meta-analysis. In: *Personnel Psychology* 57(3), pp. 639–683.

Hayes, Andrew F. (2018): Introduction to mediation, moderation and conditional process analysis. A regression-based approach. 2nd edn. New York: The Guilford Press.

Heckman, James J.; Ichimura, Hidehiko; Todd, Petra E. (1997): Matching as an econometric evaluation estimator: Evidence from evaluating a job training programme. In: *The Review of Economic Studies* 64 (4), pp. 605–654.

Heider, F. (1958): The psychology of interpersonal relations, New York: John Wiley & Sons.

Heiman, Amir; McWilliams, Bruce; Shen, Zhihua; Zilberman, David (2001): Learning and forgetting: Modeling optimal product sampling over time. In: *Management Science* 47 (4), pp. 532–546.

Helm, Roland; Hegenbart, Thomas; Endres, Herbert (2013): Explaining costumer reactions to real stockouts. In: *Review of Managerial Science* 7 (3), pp. 223–246.

Henseler, Jörg; Fassott, Georg (2010): Testing moderating effects in PLS path models: An illustration of available procedures. In: Vincenzo Esposito Vinzi, Wynne W. Chin, Jörg Henseler and Huiwen Wang (eds.): Handbook of partial least squares. Concepts, methods and applications. Berlin Heidelberg: Springer, pp. 713–735.

Hinz, Oliver; Skiera, Bernd; Barrot, Christian; Becker, Jan U. (2011): Seeding strategies for viral marketing: An empirical comparison. In: *Journal of Marketing* 75 (6), pp. 55–71.

Hirano, Keisuke; Imbens, Guido W.; Ridder, Geert (2003): Efficient estimation of average treatment effects using the estimated propensity score. In: *Econometrica* 71 (4), pp. 1161–1189.

Homburg, Christian; Giering, Annette (1996): Konzeptualisierung und Operationalisierung komplexer Konstrukte. Ein Leitfaden für die Marketingforschung. In: *Marketing ZFP* 18 (1), pp. 5–24.

Horvath, Michael; Ryan, Ann Marie; Stierwalt, Sandra L. (2000): The influence of explanations for selection test use, outcome favorability, and self-efficacy on test-taker perceptions. In: *Organizational Behavior and Human Decision Processes* 83 (2), pp. 310–330.

Howard, Daniel J. (1990): The influence of verbal responses to common greetings on compliance behavior: The foot-in-the-mouth effect. In: *Journal of Applied Social Psychology* 20 (14), pp. 1185–1196.

Hu, Nan; Liu, Ling; Bose, Indranil; Shen, Jialie (2010): Does sampling influence customers in online retailing of digital music? In: *Information Systems and E-Business Management* 8 (4), pp. 357–377.

Hu, Zhineng; Pei, Yurong; Xie, Ruikun (2014): Analysis of product sampling for new product diffusion incorporating multiple-unit ownership. In: *Hindawi Publishing Corporation*, pp. 1–10.

Huang, Qingyi; Nijs, Vincent R.; Hansen, Karsten; Anderson, Eric T. (2012): Wal-Mart's Impact on Supplier Profits. In: *Journal of Marketing Research* 49 (2), pp. 131–143.

Hulland, John (1999): Use of partial least squares (PLS) in strategic management research: A review of four recent studies. In: *Strategic Management Journal* 20 (2), pp. 195–204.

Jain, Dipak; Mahajan, Vijay; Muller, Eitan (1995): An approach for determining optimal product sampling for the diffusion of a new product. In: *Journal of Product Innovation Management: An International Publication of the Product Development & Management Association* 12 (2), pp. 124–135.

Janakiraman, Ramkumar; Lim, Joon Ho; Rishika, Rishika (2018): The effect of a data breach announcement on customer behaviour: Evidence from a multichannel retailer. In: *Journal of Marketing* 82 (2), pp. 85–105.

Jayachandran, Satish; Hewett, Kelly; Kaufman, Peter (2004): Customer response capability in a sense-and-respond era: The role of customer knowledge process. In: *Journal of the Academy of Marketing Science* 32 (3), pp. 219–233.

Jones, Edward E.; Davis, Keith (1965): From acts to dispositions: The attribution process in person perception. In: *Advances in experimental social psychology* (2), New York, pp. 219–266.

Kalra, Ajay; Shi¸ Mengze (2010): Consumer value-maximizing sweepstakes and contests. In: *Journal of Marketing Research* 47 (2), pp. 287–300.

Kelley, Harold H. (1973): The processes of causal attribution. In: *American Psychologist* 28 (2), pp. 107–128.

Kim, Eunsoo; Ding, MengQi (Annie); Wang, Xin (Shane); Lu, Shijie (2023): Does Topic Consistency Matter? A Study of Critic and User Reviews in the Movie Industry.In: *Journal of Marketing* 87(3), pp. 428–450.

Kirmani, Amna (1997): Advertising repetition as a signal of quality: If it's advertised so much, something must be wrong. In: *Journal of Advertising* 26 (3), pp. 77–86.

Klandt, Heinz; Heidenreich, Sven (2017): Empirische Forschungsmethoden in der Betriebswirtschaftslehre: Von der Forschungsfrage zum Untersuchungsdesign, eine Einführung, Berlin, Boston: De Gruyter Oldenbourg.

Ko, Hanjun; Cho, Chang-Hoan; Roberts, Marilyn S. (2005): Internet uses and gratifications: A structural equation model of interactive advertising. In: *Journal of Advertising* 34 (2), pp. 57–70.

Koschate, Nicole (2008): Experimentelle Marktforschung. In: Andreas Herrmann, Christian Homburg and Martin Klarmann (eds.): Handbuch Marktforschung. Methoden – Anwendungen – Praxisbeispiele. 3rd edn. Wiesbaden: Gabler, pp. 107–121.

Koschate-Fischer, Nicole; Schandelmeier, Stephen (2014): A guideline for designing experimental studies in marketing research and a critical discussion of selected problem areas. In: *Journal of Business Economics* 84 (6), pp. 793–826.

Koslow, Scott (2000): Can the Truth Hurt? How Honest and Persuasive Advertising Can Unintentionally Lead to Increased Consumer Skepticism. In: *The Journal of Consumer Affairs* 34 (2), pp. 245–267.

Kreis, Henning; Wildner, Raimund; Kuß, Alfred (2021): Marktforschung – Datenerhebung und Datenanalyse, 7th edn., Wiesbaden: Springer.

Kuckartz, Udo (2014): Mixed Methods. Methodologie, Forschungsdesigns und Analyseverfahren. Wiesbaden: Springer VS.

Kumar, Ashish; Bezawada, Ram; Rishika, Rishika; Janakiraman, Ramkumar; Kannan, P.K. (2016): From social to sale: The effects of firm-generated content in social media on customer behavior. In: *Journal of Marketing* 80 (1), pp. 7–25.

Kumar, Vita; Aksoy, Lerzan; Donkers, Bas; Venkatesan, Rajkumar; Wiesel, Thorsten; Tillmanns, Sebastian (2010): Undervalued or Overvalued Customers: Capturing Total Customer Engagement Value. In: Journal of Service Research 13(3), pp. 297–310.

Kuckartz, U. (2016): Qualitative Inhaltsanalyse. Methoden, Praxis, Computerunterstützung, 5th edn., Weinheim: Beltz Juventa.

Lamnek, Siegfried; Krell, Claudia (2016): Qualitative Sozialforschung. Mit Online-Material. 6th edn. Weinheim, Basel: Beltz Verlag.

Leary, Mark R. (2001): Interpersonal rejection. New York: Oxford University Press.

Leary, Mark R.; Twenge, Jean M.; Quinlivan, Erin (2006): Interpersonal rejection as a determinant of anger and aggression. In: *Personality and Social Psychology Review* 10 (2), pp. 111–132.

Leclercq, Thomas; Hammedi, Wafa; Poncin, Ingrid (2018): The boundaries of gamification for engaging customers: Effects of losing a contest in online co-creation communities. In: *Journal of Interactive Marketing* 44 (1), pp. 82–101.

Li, Hongshuang; Jain, Sanjay; Kannan, P. K. (2019): Optimal design of free samples for digital products and services. In: *Journal of Marketing Research* 56 (3), pp. 419–438.

Libai, Barak; Muller, Eitan; Peres, Renana (2013): Decomposing the value of word-of-mouth seeding programs: Acceleration versus expansion. In: *Journal of Marketing Research* 50 (2), pp. 161–176.

Lokhorst, Anne Marike; Werner, Carol; Staats, Henk; van Dijk, Eric; Gale, Jeff L. (2013): Commitment and Behavior Change: A Meta-Analysis and Critical Review of Commitment-Making Strategies in Environmental Research. In: *Environment and Behavior* 45 (1), pp. 3–34

Lu, Xianghua; Phang, Chee Wei; Ba, Sulin; Yao, Xinlin (2018): Know who to give: Enhancing the effectiveness of online product sampling. In: *Decision Support Systems* 105, pp. 77–86.

Macan, Therese H.; Avedon, Marcia J.; Paese, Matthew; Smith, David E. (1994): The effects of applicants' reactions to cognitive ability tests and an assessment center. In: *Personnel Psychology* 47 (4), pp. 715–738.

Marks, Lawrence J.; Kamins, Michael A. (1988): The use of product sampling and advertising: Effects of sequence of exposure and degree of advertising claim exaggeration on consumers' belief strength, belief confidence, and attitudes. In: *Journal of Marketing Research* 25 (3), pp. 266–281.

Mayring, Philipp (2023): Einführung in die qualitative Sozialforschung, 7th edn., Weinheim Basel: Beltz.

McDonald, Melissa M.; Donnellan, M. Brent (2012): Is ostracism a strong situation? The influence of personality in reactions to rejection. In: *Journal of Research in Personality* 46 (5), pp. 614–618.

MediaMarkt (2023): MediaMarkt Produkttester-Community, online verfügbar unter: https://www.mediamarkt.de/de/campaign/testpiloten, Accessed: 04.09.2023.

Mende, Martin; Bolton, Ruth N.; Bitner, Mary Jo (2013): Decoding Customer–Firm Relationships: How Attachment Styles Help Explain Customers' Preferences for Closeness, Repurchase Intentions, and Changes in Relationship Breadth. In: *Journal of Marketing Research* 50(1), pp. 125–142.

Mey, Günter; Mruck, Katja (2011): Qualitative Interviews. In: Naderer, Gabriele; Balzer, Vea (eds.). Qualitative Marktforschung in Theorie und Praxis – Grundlagen – Methoden – Anwendungen, 2nd edn., Wiesbaden: Springer, pp. 257–288.

Moriarty, Thomas (1975): Crime, commitment, and the responsive bystander: Two field experiments. In: *Journal of Personality and Social Psychology* 31 (2), pp. 370–376.

Müller, E.; Moser, K. (2006): Reaktionen auf Ablehnungsschreiben an Bewerber: Das Beispiel „Eisschreiben". In: *German Journal of Human Resource Management* 20 (4), pp. 343–355.

Muraven, Mark; Tice, Dianne M.; Baumeister, Roy F. (1998): Self-control as limited resource: Regulatory depletion patterns. In: *Journal of Personality and Social Psychology* 74 (3), pp. 774–789.

Nejad, Mohammad G.; Amini, Mehdi; Babakus, Emin (2015): Success factors in product seeding: The role of homophily. In: *Journal of Retailing* 91 (1), pp. 68–88.

Netemeyer, Richard G.; Maxham III, James G.; Pullig, Chris (2005): Conflicts in the Work-Family Interface: Links to Job Stress, Customer Service Employee Performance, and Customer Purchase Intent, in: *Journal of Marketing* 69 (2), pp. 130–143.

Nunnally, Jum C. (1978): Psychometric theory. 2nd edn., New York: McGraw-Hill.

Oliver, Richard L. (2010): Satisfaction: A behavioral perspective on the consumer, 2nd edn., New York, Routledge.

Onoda, Keiichi; Okamoto, Yasumasa; Nakashima, Ken'ichiro; Nittono, Hiroshi; Yoshimura, Shinpei; Yamawaki, Sigeto; Yamaguchi, Shuhei; Ura, Mitsuhiro (2010): Does low self-esteem enhance social pain? The relationship between trait self-esteem and anterior cingulate cortex activation induced by ostracism. In: *Social Cognitive and Affective Neuroscience* 5 (4), pp. 385–391.

Palan, Stefan; Schitter, Christian (2018): Prolific.ac – A subject pool for online experiments. In: *Journal of Behavioral and Experimental Finance* 17, pp. 22–27.

Palmatier, Robert W.; Dant, Rajiv P.; Grewal, Dhruv; Evans, Kenneth R. (2006): Factors influencing the effectiveness of relationship marketing: A meta-analysis. In: *Journal of Marketing* 70 (4), pp. 136–153.

Park, Cheol Whee; Macinnis, Deborah J.; Priester, Joseph; Eisingerich, Andreas B.; Iacobucci, Dawn (2010): Brand Attachment and Brand Attitude Strength: Conceptual and Empirical Differentiation of Two Critical Brand Equity Drivers.In: *Journal of Marketing*, 74 (6), pp. 1–17.

Parkinson, Brian (2007): Soziale Wahrnehmung und Attribution. In: Wolfgang Stroebe, Klaus Jonas and Miles Hewstone (eds.): Sozialpsychologie. Eine Einführung. 5th edn. Heidelberg: Springer Medizin Verlag, pp. 69–109.

Patry, Jean-Luc (1982): Feldforschung: Methoden und Probleme sozialwissenschaftlicher Forschung unter natürlichen Bedingungen, Bern: Huber.

Paul, Karsten; Moser, Klaus (2001): Negatives psychisches Befinden als Wirkung und als Ursache von Arbeitslosigkeit: Ergebnisse einer Metaanalyse. In: Jeannette Zempel, Johann Bacher and Klaus Moser (eds.): Erwerbslosigkeit. Ursachen, Auswirkungen und Interventionen. Wiesbaden: Springer Fachmedien, pp. 83–110.

Peterson, Christopher; Seligman, Martin E. P. (1984): Causal explanations as a risk factor for depression: Theory and evidence. In: *Psychological Review* 91 (3), pp. 347–374.

Philips (2023): Philips Produkttester-Community, online verfügbar unter: https://www.philips.de/c-e/produkttester-werden.html, Accessed 04.09.2023.

Piezunka, Henning; Dahlander, Linus (2019): Idea rejected, tie formed: Organizations' feedback on crowdsourced ideas. In: *Academy of Management Journal* 62 (2), pp. 503–530.

Ployhart, Robert E.; Ryan, Ann Marie (1997): Toward an explanation of applicant reactions: An examination of organizational justice and attribution frameworks. In: *Organizational Behavior and Human Decision Processes* 72 (3), pp. 308–335.

Putrevu, Sanjay; Tan, Joni; Lord, Kenneth R. (2004): Consumer responses to complex advertisements: The moderating role of need for cognition, knowledge, and gender. In: *Journal of Current Issues & Research in Advertising* 26 (1), pp. 9–24.

Rafaeli, Anat (1999): Pre-employment screening and applicants' attitudes toward an employment opportunity. In: *The Journal of Social Psychology* 139 (6), pp. 700–712.

Rehman, Shafique Ur; Bhatti, Anam; Mohamed, Rapiah; Ayoup, Hazeline (2019): The moderating role of trust and commitment between consumer purchase intention and online shopping behavior in the context of Pakistan. In: Journal of Global Entrepreneurship Research 9(43), pp. 1–25.

Reinecke, Sven; Tomczak, Torsten (2006): Handbuch Marketing-Controlling – Effektivität und Effizienz einer marktorientierten Unternehmensführung, 2nd edn., Gabler.

REWE (2023): REWE Produkttester-Community, online verfügbar unter: https://produkttests.rewe.de/, Accessed: 04.09.2023.

Rishika, Rishika; Kumar, Ashish; Janakiraman, Ramkumar; Bezawada, Ram (2013): The effect of customers' social media participation on customer visit frequency and profitability: An empirical investigation. In: *Information Systems Research* 24 (1), pp. 108–127.

Rosenbaum, Paul R.; Rubin, Donald B. (1985): Constructing a control group using multivariate matched sampling methods that incorporate the propensity score. In: *The American Statistician* 39 (1), pp. 33–38.

Rubin, Donald B.; Stuart, Elizabeth A. (2006): Affinely invariant matching methods with discriminant mixtures of proportional ellipsoidally symmetric distributions. In: *The Annals of Statistics* 34 (4), pp. 1814–1826.

Rubin, Donald B.; Thomas, Neal (1996): Matching using estimated propensity scores: Relating theory to practice. In: *Biometrics* 52 (1), pp. 249–264.

Rudert, Selma C.; Greifeneder, Rainer (2016): When it's okay that I don't play: Social norms and the situated construal of social exclusion. In: *Personality and Social Psychology Bulletin* 42 (7), pp. 955–969.

Rust, Roland T.; Lemon, Katherine N.; Zeithaml, Valarie A. (2004): Return on Marketing: Using Customer Equity to Focus Marketing Strategy. In: *Journal of Marketing* 68(1), pp. 109–127

Ryan, Ann Marie; Ployhart, Robert E. (2000): Applicants' perceptions of selection procedures and decisions: A critical review and agenda for the future. In: *Journal of Management* 26 (3), pp. 565–606.

Sanchez-Ruiz, Lidia; Blanco, Beatriz; Kyguolienė, Asta (2018): A theoretical overview of the stockout problem in retail: From causes to consequences. In: *Management of Organizations: Systematic Research* 79 (1), pp. 103–116.

Sautmann, Stefan (2016): Mundpropaganda 2.0. Wie Unternehmen die „Macht des Empfehlens" als Geschäftsmodelle etablieren. In: *Zeitschrift Führung + Organisation* 85 (3), pp. 174–179.

Schlereth, Christian; Barrot, Christian; Skiera, Bernd; Takac, Carsten (2013): Optimal product-sampling strategies in social networks: How many and whom to target? In: *International Journal of Electronic Commerce* 18 (1), pp. 45–72.

Schnell, Rainer; Hill, Paul B.; Esser, Elke (2011): Methoden der empirischen Sozialforschung. 9th edn., München: Oldenbourg.

Shapiro, Debra L.; Buttner, E. Holly; Barry, Bruce (1994): Explanations: What factors enhance their perceived adequacy? In: *Organizational Behavior and Human Decision Processes* 58 (3), pp. 346–368.

Sherman, Steven J. (1980): On the self-erasing nature of errors of prediction. In: *Journal of Personality and Social Psychology* 39 (2), pp. 211–221.

Silverman, Bernard W. (1986): Density estimation for statistics and data analysis. London: Chapman and Hall.

Smith, Robert E.; Swinyard, William R. (1983): Attitude-behavior consistency: The impact of product trial versus advertising. In: *Journal of Marketing Research* 20 (3), pp. 257–267.

Smither, James W.; Reilly, Richard R.; Millsap, Roger E.; Pearlman, Kenneth; Stoffey, Ronald W. (1993): Applicant reactions to selection procedures. In: *Personnel Psychology* 46 (1), pp. 49–76.

Sprott, David E.; Shimp, Terence A. (2004): Using product sampling to augment the perceived quality of store brands. In: *Journal of Retailing* 80 (4), pp. 305–315.

Staples-Otis, Laura (2022). Product sampling marketing: When, why, and how to do it, The Bazaar Voice, online verfügbar unter: https://www.bazaarvoice.com/blog/product-sampling-marketing/, Accessed: 04.09.2023.

Steinhoff, Lena (2014): Loyalitätswirkung des geschenkten bevorzugten Kundenstatus. Eine theoretische und empirisch-experimentelle Analyse. Wiesbaden: Springer Gabler.

Steinhoff, Lena; Palmatier, Robert W. (2016): Understanding loyalty program effectiveness: Managing target and bystander effects. In: *Journal of the Academy of Marketing Science* 44, pp. 88–107.

Strauss, Anselm L. (1998): Grundlagen qualitativer Sozialforschung. Datenanalyse und Theoriebil-dung in der empirischen soziologischen Forschung (2nd edn.). München: Wilhelm Fink Verlag.

Stroebe, Wolfgang; Jonas, Klaus; Hewstone, Miles (2003): Sozialpsychologie: Eine Einführung. 4th edn. Berlin Heidelberg: Springer.

Stuart, Elizabeth A. (2010): Matching methods for causal inference: A review and a look forward. In: *Statistical Science* 25 (1), pp. 1–21.

Suh, Jung-Chae; Yi, Youjae (2006): When brand attitudes affect the customer satisfaction-loyalty relation: The moderating role of product involvement. In: *Journal of Consumer Psychology* 16 (2), pp. 145–155.

Suri, Rajneesh; Kohli, Chiranjeev; Monroe, Kent. B. (2007): The effects of perceived scarcity on consumers' processing of price information. In: *Journal of the Academy of Marketing Science* 35(*1*), pp. 89–100

Tokman, Mert; Davis, Lenita M.; Lemon, Katherine N. (2007): The wow factor: Creating value through win-back offers to reacquire lost customers. In: *Journal of Retailing* 83 (1), pp. 47–64.

trnd (2023): Ablauf Produkttests – online verfügbar unter: https://www.trnd.com/de/, Accessed: 02.09.2023.

Urbany, Joel E.; Dickson, Peter R.; Wilkie, William L. (1989): Buyer Uncertainty and Information Search. In: *Journal of Consumer Research*, 16(2), pp. 208–215.

Walker, H. Jack; Helmut, Catherine A.; Field, Hubert S.; Bauer, Talya N. (2015): Watch what you say: Job applicants' justice perceptions from initial organizational correspondence. In: *Human Resource Management, 54*(6), pp. 999–1 011.

Wang, Ting; Oh, Lih-Bin; Wang, Kanliang; Yuan, Yufei (2013): User adoption and purchasing intention after free trial: an empirical study of mobile newspapers. In: *Information Systems and E-Business Management* 11 (2), pp. 189–210.

Wangenheim, Florian v.; Bayón, Tomás (2007): Behavioral consequences of overbooking service capacity. In: *Journal of Marketing* 71 (4), pp. 36–47.

Ward, James C.; Hill, Ronald P.; Gardner, Meryl P. (1988): Promotional games: The effects of participation on mood, attitude, and information processing. In: *Advances in Consumer Research* 15 (1), pp. 135–140.

Ward, James C.; Hill, Ronald P. (1991): Designing effective promotional games: Opportunities and problems. In: *Journal of Advertising* 20 (3), pp. 69–81.

Weiner, Bernard (1979): A theory of motivation for some classroom experiences. In: *Journal of Educational Psychology* 71 (1), pp. 3–25.

Weiner, Bernard (1985): An attributional theory of achievement motivation and emotion. In: *Psychological Review* 92 (4), pp. 548–573.

Weiner, Bernard (1986): An attributional theory of motivation and emotion, New York: Springer-Verlag.

Wesselmann, Eric D.; Wirth, James H.; Mroczek, Daniel K.; Williams, Kipling D. (2012): Dial a feeling: Detecting moderation of affect decline during ostracism. In: *Personality and Individual Differences* 53 (5), pp. 580–586.

Wesselmann, Eric D.; Williams, Kipling D. (2017): Social life and social death: Inclusion, ostracism, and rejection in groups. In: *Group Processes & Intergroup Relations* 20 (5), pp. 693–706.

Williams, Kipling D.; Sommer, Kristin L. (1997): Social ostracism by coworkers: Does rejection lead to loafing or compensation? In: *Personality and Social Psychology Bulletin* 23 (7), pp. 693–706.

Williams, Kipling D.; Cheung, Christopher K. T.; Choi, Wilma (2000): Cyberostracism: Effects of being ignored over the internet. In: *Journal of Personality and Social Psychology* 79 (5), pp. 748–762.

Williams, Kipling D. (2001): Ostracism: The power of silence. New York: Guilford.

Williams, Kipling D.; Zadro, Lisa (2001): Ostracism: On being ignorde, excluded, and rejected. In: Leary, Mark R. (ed.): Interpersonal rejection, New York: Oxford University Press, pp. 21–54.

Wirth, James H.; Lynam, Donald R.; Williams, Kipling D. (2010): When social pain is not automatic: Personality disorder traits buffer ostracism's immediate negative impact. In: *Journal of Research in Personality* 44 (3), pp. 397–401.

Wright, Alice A.; Lynch Jr, John G. (1995): Communication effects of advertising versus direct experience when both search and experience attributes are present. In: *Journal of Consumer Research* 21 (4), pp. 708–718.

Wu, Lingli; Deng, Shiming; Jiang, Xuan (2018): Sampling and pricing strategy under competition. In: *Omega* 80, pp. 192–208.

Yao, Xinlin; Lu, Xianghua; Phang, Chee Wei; Huang, Lihua; Ba, Sulin (2014): Administering and capitalizing on product sampling in an online context. In: *Pacific Asia Conference on Information Systems (PACIS) Proceedings*, pp. 1–14.

Yao, Xinlin; Lu, Xianghua; Phang, Chee Wei; Ba, Sulin (2017): Dynamic sales impacts of online physical product sampling. In: *Information & Management* 54 (5), pp. 599–612.

Yi, Youjae; Jeon, Hoseong (2003): Effects of loyalty programs on value perception, program loyalty, and brand loyalty. In: *Journal of the Academy of Marketing Science* 31 (3), pp. 229–240.

Zhang, Ying; Goh, Khim-Yong; Lin, Zhijie (2017): Investigating the sales spillover effects of online product sampling in e-commerce. In: *ICIS 2017 Proceedings*, pp. 1–12.

Zhou, Wenqi; Duan, Wenjing (2015): An empirical study of how third-party websites influence the feedback mechanism between online word-of-mouth and retail sales. In: *Decision Support Systems* 76, pp. 14–23.